Franz
LISZT

CE QU'ON ENTEND SUR LA MONTAGNE

Symphonic Poem No. 1

S. 95

Study Score
Partitur

PETRUCCI LIBRARY PRESS

A celle qui a accompli sa foi par l'amour —
agrandi son espérance à travers les douleurs —
édifié son bonheur dans le sacrifice —
à celle qui demeure la compagne de ma vie,
le firmament de mes pensées, la prière vivante
et le ciel de mon âme —
à Jeanne Elisabeth Carolyne
      8 Février 1855.

                                  F. Liszt.

Ihr, die ihren Glauben durch Liebe bewährte,
deren Hoffen wuchs in der Leiden Fülle,
die ihr Glück darin fand, sich zum Opfer zu bringen,
Ihr, die die Gefährtin meines Lebens,
das Sternenzelt meiner Gedanken,
das lebendige Gebet und der Himmel meiner Seele bleibt —
Jeanne Elisabeth Carolyne
      8. Februar 1855.

                                  F. Liszt.

COMPOSER'S PREFACE

Eine Aufführung, welche den Intentionen des Komponisten entsprechen und ihnen Klang, Farbe, Rhythmus und Leben verleihen soll, wird bei meinen Orchester-Werken am zweckmässigsten und mit dem geringsten Zeitverlust durch geteilte Vor-Proben gefördert werden. Demzufolge erlaube ich mir, die HH. Dirigenten, welche meine symphonischen Dichtungen aufzuführen beabsichtigen, zu ersuchen, der General-Probe Separat-Proben mit dem Streich-Quartett, andere mit Blas- und Schlag-Instrumenten vorangehen zu lassen.

Gleichzeitig sei mir gestattet zu bemerken, dass ich das mechanische, taktmässige, zerschnittene Auf- und Abspielen, wie es an manchen Orten noch üblich ist, möglichst beseitigt wünsche, und nur den periodischen Vortrag, mit dem Hervortreten der besonderen Accente und der Abrundung der melodischen und rhythmischen Nuanzierung, als sachgemäss anerkennen kann. In der geistigen Auffassung des Dirigenten liegt der Lebensnerv einer symphonischen Produktion, vorausgesetzt, dass im Orchester die geziemenden Mittel zu deren Verwirklichung sich vorfinden; andernfalls möchte es ratsamer erscheinen, sich nicht mit Werken zu befassen, welche keineswegs eine Alltags-Popularität beanspruchen.

Obschon ich bemüht war, durch genaue Anzeichnungen meine Intentionen zu verdeutlichen, so verhehle ich doch nicht, dass Manches, ja sogar das Wesentlichste, sich nicht zu Papier bringen lässt, und nur durch das künstlerische Vermögen, durch sympathisch schwungvolles Reproduzieren, sowohl des Dirigenten als der Aufführenden, zur durchgreifenden Wirkung gelangen kann. Dem Wohlwollen meiner Kunstgenossen sei es daher überlassen, das Meiste und Vorzüglichste an meinen Werken zu vollbringen.

Weimar, März 1856.

Pour obtenir un résultat d'exécution correspondant aux intentions de mes œuvres orchestrales, et leur donner le coloris, le rhythme, l'accent et la vie qu'elles réclament, il sera utile d'en préparer la répétition générale par des répétitions partielles des instruments à cordes, à vent, en cuivre, et à percussion. Par cette méthode de la division du travail on épargnera du temps en facilitant aux exécutants l'intelligence de l'ouvrage. Je me permets en conséquence de prier MM. les chefs d'orchestre qui seraient disposés à faire exécuter l'un de ces Poèmes symphoniques, de vouloir bien prendre le soin de faire précéder les répétitions générales, des répétitions préalables indiquées ci-dessus.

En même temps j'observerai que la mesure dans les œuvres de ce genre demande à être maniée avec plus de mesure, de souplesse, et d'intelligence des effets de coloris, de rhythme, et d'expression qu'il n'est encore d'usage dans beaucoup d'orchestres. Il ne suffit pas qu'une composition soit régulièrement bâtonnée et machinalement exécutée avec plus ou moins de correction pour que l'auteur ait à se louer de cette façon de propagation de son œuvre, et puisse y reconnaître une fidèle interprétation de sa pensée. Le nerf vital d'une belle exécution symphonique gît principalement dans la compréhension de l'œuvre reproduite, que le chef d'orchestre doit surtout posséder et communiquer, dans la manière de partager et d'accentuer les périodes, d'accuser les contrastes tout en ménageant les transitions de veiller tantôt à établir l'équilibre entre les divers instruments, tantôt à les faire ressortir soit isolément soit par groupes, car à tel moment il convient d'entonner ou de marquer simplement les notes, mais à d'autres il s'agit de phraser, de chanter, et même de déclamer. C'est au chef qu'il appartient d'indiquer à chacun des membres de l'orchestre la signification du rôle qu'il a à remplir.

Je me suis attaché à rendre mes intentions par rapport aux nuances, à l'accélération et au retard des mouvements, etc. aussi sensibles que possible par un emploi détaillé des signes et des expressions usitées; néanmoins ce serait une illusion de croire qu'on puisse fixer sur le papier ce qui fait la beauté et le caractère de l'exécution. Le talent et l'inspiration des artistes dirigeants et exécutants en ont seuls le secret, et la part de sympathie que ceux-ci voudront bien accorder à mes œuvres, seront pour elles le meilleur gage de succès.

Weimar, Mars 1856.

In order to secure a performance of my orchestral works which accords with their intentions, and which imparts to them the colour, rhythm, accent and life that they require, it is recommended that the general rehearsal should be preceded by separate rehearsals of the Strings, Wind, Brass, and instruments of percussion. By this division of labour time will be saved, and the executants will more rapidly be made familiar with what is required of them. I therefore venture to request that conductors, who are pleased to bring one or the other of my symphonic poems to a hearing will adopt the plan formulated above.

At the same time I may be allowed to remark that it is my wish that the mechanical, bar by bar, up and down beating of time, which obtains in so many places, should as far as possible be discarded, and that only the periodic divisions, with the prominence of certain accentuation and the rounding off of melodic and rhythmical nuances should alone be regarded as indispensable. The vitality of a symphonic performance depends upon the intellectual perception of the conductor, presuming that suitable material for its realisation is to be found in the orchestra; failing this it would seem to be advisable to hold aloof from works which do not claim a promise of every-day popularity.

Although I have endeavoured to make my intentions clear by providing exact marks of expression, I cannot conceal from myself that much, and that perhaps the most important, cannot be set forth on paper, but can only be successfully brought to light by the artistic capability and the sympathetic and enthusiastic reproduction by both conductor and executants. It may therefore be left to my colleagues in art to do the most and best that they can for my works.

Weimar, March 1856.

F. Liszt.

INTRODUCTION

The present score is a reissue of one from the Franz Liszt-Stiftung edition, originally published by Breitkopf & Härtel from 1907-1936. The edition was prepared in an effort to publish the entire oeuvre of Franz Liszt. Editors included such prominent musicians as Béla Bartok, Ferruccio Busoni, Eugène d'Albert and José Vianna da Motta – some of whom studied with Liszt – as well as scholars like Peter Raabe, who would later compile the first catalog of the composer's works. The need for a complete edition was already apparent by the time of Liszt's death. Although some of his piano music had regularly appeared in new editions throughout his life, these works were by no means representative of even his pianistic output. A far more unfortunate fate was left for his orchestral music - which would usually be issued only once, soon to go out of print and later scarcely available. The Liszt-Stiftung edition revived many works that had fallen into relative obscurity and was therefore handsomely welcomed.

The edition was sadly never completed. The publication activity was brought to a premature end by the time of the Second World War. All in all the incomplete edition encompassed 34 volumes, among others two symphonies, the symphonic poems, some concert works, a couple of piano arrangements and 11 volumes of original works for piano – a mere fraction of the composer's output – but the edition would nonetheless break the ground for Liszt research during the 20th century for a number of reasons. First, it brought to light a number of late pieces that would put Liszt as a forerunner of experimental music and firmly establish his position as such. Second, it revealed the diversity of Liszt's output, which up until that time had been best known as an important addition to the piano repertoire. Third, it displayed the complex and characteristic nature of many of his works by being the first edition to show and make use of several alternative (sometimes vastly different) versions and sources. Last but not least, it would provide the world with a generally reliable edition of easy availability and very high standard for its day.

The Bavarian State Library acquired a complete copy of said edition and decided to digitize it in 2008. By that time more than 70 years had passed since its publication, effectively rendering the edition out of copyright and free for any use. Each and every page was scanned and uploaded to their online digital collection. While this was a great effort in itself, the site has a rudimentary interface, is difficult to navigate and the scores are not in the context of relevant information. One of our users decided to also upload it to our site, the International Music Score Library Project (IMSLP) / Petrucci Music Library, the unique wiki-based repository of musical scores, composers and indexes that anyone can edit and amend. Through the effort of a single user, Mattias K. (piupianissimo), the entire edition is now easily available worldwide to those who wish to perform and study the composer's music in a historical context, since as the case is with Liszt's music, many early editions exist and many are readily available on the site and many more will be available in the future. IMSLP is as such a valuable resource available to the scholar but even more to the performer who is always a mere mouse click away from scores that have not been in print since the turn of the past century, or that are otherwise hard to come by. The availability, quantity of ease of access for online scores will soon exceed those of the traditional medium of print. Nevertheless new works have always been published through the printed medium and this tradition is going to persist for many years to come even if complemented by the digital medium. Of course an important fact to stress is that the availability of digital scores online does not exclude the need of printed score since neither one can replace the comfort and neatness of one another. The quality of a bound reprint or new engraving exceeds that of a score printed at home.

I discovered IMSLP back in early 2006 when it first began. At that time many scores were scattered on the net either privately or on commercial collection sites. Many of these sites had a considerably large collection but sadly many had restrictions on number of downloads per day and the process of contributing to them was riddled with bureaucracy. IMSLP was the first free site where anyone could contribute and upload any kind of musical scores. I have personally searched and uploaded many works – particularly those of Liszt – and the future of the site is nothing but bright. At the time of its start only a handful of scores were available on the site but through the effort of its users IMSLP has grown to be the largest collection of scores available on the Internet.

Ce qu'on entend sue la montagne is the first work in a series of thirteen symphonic poems composed by Franz Liszt. It was composed from 1848-54 and first published in 1857 by Breitkopf und Härtel of Leipzig. The dedicatee is Princess Carolyne zu Sayn-Wittgenstein. The present score is reproduced from the first volume of the Franz Liszt-Stiftung edition which was edited by Otto Taubmann and originally published in 1908. A scan of the 1908 score, along with a number of arrangements, is also available for free download at the following URL:

http:// imslp.org/wiki/Ce_qu%27on_entend_sur_la_montagne,_S.95_(Liszt,_Franz)

Soren Afshar (Funper)

Summer, 2011

WAS MAN AUF DEM BERGE HÖRT.

SYMPHONISCHE DICHTUNG No. 1 VON F. LISZT.

O altitudo!

Seid ihr wohl zuweilen ernst und still
Auf einen Berg gestiegen, nah den Himmeln?
An Sundes Ufern? an Bretagnes Küsten?
Saht ihr das Meer zu eures Berges Füssen?
Dort über Wogen, über Unermess'nes
Euch neigend, habt ihr ernst und still gelauscht?

Das hört man: — ich wenigstens, als träumend
Mein Geist den Flug gelenket auf ein Ufer,
Und, sich vom Gipfel in den Abgrund senkend,
Die Erde dort und dort das Meer ersah,
Ich lauschte, hörte, was aus keinem Munde
Jemals ertönte, noch ein Ohr bewegt.

Zuerst verworr'ner, unermess'ner Lärm,
Undeutlich, wie der Wind in dichten Bäumen,
Voll klarer Töne, süssen Lispelns, sanft
Wie'n Abendlied, und stark wie Waffenklirren,
Wenn dumpf das Treffen die Schwadronen mischt,
Und wütend stösst in der Trompete Mündung.
Es war ein Tönen, tief und unaussprechlich,
Das, flutend, Kreise zog rings um die Welt,
Und durch die Himmel, welche seine Wogen
Verjüngt, rollend sein unendlich Wort
Verbreitete, bis wo es in den Schatten
Mit Zeit, Raum, Zahl, Gestaltung überging!
Ein andrer Luftkreis, weit und fessellos,
Umgab die Erde ganz der ew'ge Hymnus.
Die Welt, gehüllt in diese Symphonie,
Schwamm, wie in Luft, so in der Harmonie.

Und sinnend lauscht ich diesen Ätherharfen,
Verloren in der Stimme, wie im Meer.
Bald unterschied ich, noch verwirrt, verschleiert,
Gemischt zwei Stimmen in der einen Stimme,
Vor Erd' und Meeren in den Himmel steigend,
Ich schied sie deutlich in dem Lärm, wie man
Zwei Ströme sieht sich unter Wogen kreuzen.

CE QU'ON ENTEND SUR LA MONTAGNE.

POÈME SYMPHONIQUE No. 1 DE F. LISZT.

O altitudo!

Avez-vous quelquefois, calme et silencieux,
Monté sur la montagne, en présence des cieux?
Était-ce aux bords du Sund? aux côtes de
Bretagne?
Aviez-vous l'océan au pied de la montagne?
Et là, penché sur l'onde et sur l'immensité,
Calme et silencieux avez-vous écouté?

Voici ce qu'on entend: — du moins un jour
qu'en rêve
Ma pensée abattit son vol sur une grève,
Et du sommet d'un mont plongeant au gouffre
amer,
Vit d'un côté la terre et de l'autre la mer,
J'écoutai, j'entendis, et jamais voix pareille
Ne sortit d'une bouche et n'émut une oreille.

Ce fut d'abord un bruit large, immense, confus,
Plus vague que le vent dans les arbres touffus,
Plein d'accords éclatants, de suaves murmures,
Doux comme un chant du soir, fort comme un
choc d'armures
Quand la sourde mêlée étreint les escadrons,
Et souffle, furieuse, aux bouches des clairons.
C'était une musique ineffable et profonde,
Qui, fluide, oscillait sans cesse autour du monde,
Et dans les vastes cieux, par ses flots rajeunis,
Roulait élargissant ses orbes infinis
Jusqu'au fond où son flux s'allait perdre dans
l'ombre
Avec le temps, l'espace et la forme et le nombre!
Comme une autre atmosphère épars et débordé,
L'hymne éternel couvrait tout le globe inondé.
Le monde enveloppé dans cette symphonie,
Comme il vogue dans l'air, voguait dans l'har-
monie.

Et pensif, j'écoutais ces harpes de l'éther,
Perdu dans cette voix comme dans une mer.

Bientôt je distinguai, confuses et voilées,
Deux voix dans cette voix l'une à l'autre mêlées,
De la terre et des mers s'épanchant jusqu'au ciel,
Qui chantaient à la fois le chant universel;
Et je les distinguai dans la rumeur profonde
Comme on voit deux courants qui se croisent
sous l'onde.

WHAT ONE HEARS ON THE MOUNTAINS

SYMPHONIC POEM No. 1 BY F. LISZT.

O altitudo!

Silent and calm, have you e'er scaled the height
Of some lone mountain peak, in heaven's sight?
Was it beside the Sund, or Breton shore,
Where ocean stretched the mountain's feet before?
Bent o'er the deep and boundless space, to hear —
Silent and calm — have you inclined your ear?

'Tis this we hear — at least, in dreams, one day
My thought did on the strand its pinions stay,
And from a beetling cliff, on either hand
Gazed on the ocean world, and bounding land,
I listened, heard, and such a voice did ne'er,
From such a mouth, strike upon mortal ear!

First, 'twas a voice, immense, vast, undefined,
More vague than through the forest sounds the
wind;
Full of harsh notes — soft murmurs, full of charms,
Sweet as night music, strong as clash of arms,
When squadrons meet in furious fight, and fast,
While the loud clarions blow their fatal blast.

Music it was, ineffable and deep,
Which vibrates, flows, and round the world doth
sweep,
And in the skies immense, its waves makes young
In large and larger orbits rolls along;
Till in the depth its billows reach the shade
Where time, space, number, form, are lost and
fade.
Like a new atmosphere through space dispersed,
Th' eternal hymn the total globe immersed:
The world, encompassed in that symphony,
As though the air did through that music fly,
Thus by th' eternal harps thought-bound, I stood,
Lost in the voice as in the ocean's flood.

Soon with that voice confusedly combined,
Two other voices, vague and veiled, I find.
The earth, the seas poured forth to heaven
their cry,
Which sang the universal harmony,
And seemed each voice, though mixed, distinct
to be,

Vom Meer die eine; Ruhmes-Glückslied!
Die Wogen sprachen also zu einander;
Die and're hob von unsrer Erde sich,
Sie war voll Trauer — das Geräusch der Menschen;
Und in dies Lied, das Tag und Nacht nicht schweigt,
Klingt jede Welle mit und jeder Mensch.

Der prächt'ge Ozean — ich sagt' es schon —
Liess eine friedlich frohe Stimme hören,
Sang, wie die Harfe singt in Sions Tempeln.
Und pries der Schöpfung Schönheit. Sein Getöse
Ward mitgenommen von des Windes Wogen,
Stieg ungesäumt, wie im Triumph zu Gott,
Und — welche Gott nur zähmt — der Wellen jede
Fing, wenn die and're schwieg zu singen an.
Zuweilen liess das Meer, wie Daniels Gast,
Der grosse Leu, die laute Stimme sinken;
Und unter seinen goldnen Mähnen glaubt' ich
Im Flammenabend Gottes Hand zu seh'n.

Doch unter diesen hehren Klängen schrillte
Die and're Stimme, wie ein ängstlich Ross,
Wie einer Höllenpforte rost'ge Angel,
Wie ehr'ner Bogen auf der Eisenlaute.
Und Schreien, Weinen, Schmähen und Verfluchen,
Der Taufe Weig'rung und des letzten Mahles,
Und Fluch und Lästerung und wild Geschrei
Taucht' aus des Menschenlärmes Wirbelwogen,
Wie man des Abends in den Thälern schwarze
Nachtvögel sieht, die schaarenweise ziehen.
Was war dies Rauschen, endlos widerhallend?
Der Mensch, ach! und die Erde, welche weinten.

Die wundersamen unerhörten Stimmen,
Stets wiederkehrend nnd verschwindend, die
In alle Ewigkeit der Ew'ge hört;
Die eine sprach: Natur! die and're: Menschheit!

Da dacht' ich nach — noch hatte leider nie
Zum grössern Schwunge sich mein Geist entfaltet,
Nie schien noch in mein Dunkel solches Licht, —
Da träumt' ich lange, wechselweis' betrachtend
Nach jenem Abgrund, den die Wellen bargen.
Den tiefern, der in mir sich öffnete.
Ich fragte mich, warum man hier ist, was
Der Zweck von allem diesem endlich, was
Die Seele thut, ob Sein, ob Leben besser,
Und warum Gott, der einzig lies't sein Buch,
Beständig einet zu des Liedes Misston
Sang der Natur mit seinen Menschen Schreien.

L'une venait des mers; chant de gloire! hymne
heureux!
C'était la voix des flots qui se parlaient entre eux;
L'autre, qui s'élevait de la terre où nous sommes,
Était triste: c'était le murmure des hommes;
Et dans ce grand concert, qui chantait jour et nuit,
Chaque onde avait sa voix et chaque homme
son bruit.

Or, comme je l'ai dit, l'océan magnifique
Épandait une voix joyeuse et pacifique,
Chantait comme la harpe aux temples de Sion,
Et louait la beauté de la création.
Sa clameur, qu'emportaient la brise et la rafale,
Incessamment vers Dieu montait plus triomphale,
Et chacun de ces flots, que Dieu seul peut
dompter,
Quand l'autre avait fini, se levait pour chanter.
Comme ce grand lion dont Daniel fut l'hôte,
L'océan par moments abaissait sa voix haute,
Et moi, je croyais voir, vers le couchant en feu,
Sous sa crinière d'or passer la main de Dieu.

Cependant, à côté de l'auguste fanfare,
L'autre voix, comme un cri de coursier qui
s'effare,
Comme le gond rouillé d'une porte d'enfer,
Comme l'archet d'airain sur la lyre de fer,
Grinçait: et pleurs, et cris, l'injure, l'anathème,
Refus du viatique et refus du baptême,
Et malédiction, et blasphème, et clameur,
Dans le flot tournoyant de l'humaine rumeur,
Passaient, comme le soir on voit dans les vallées
De noirs oiseaux de nuit qui s'en vont par volées.
Qu'était-ce que ce bruit dont mille échos vibraient?
Hélas! c'étaient la terre et l'homme qui pleuraient.

Frères! de ces deux voix étranges, inouïes,
Sans cesse renaissant, sans cesse évanouies,
Qu'écoute l'Eternel durant l'éternité,
L'une disait: Nature! et l'autre: Humanité!

Alors je méditai; car mon esprit fidèle,
Hélas! n'avait jamais déployé plus grande aile;
Dans mon ombre jamais n'avait lui tant de jour;
Et je rêvais longtemps, contemplant tour à tour,
Après l'abîme obscur que me cachait la lame,
L'autre abîme sans fond qui s'ouvrait dans mon
âme.
Et je me demandai pourquoi l'on est ici,
Quel peut être après tout le but de tout ceci,
Que fait l'âme, lequel vaut mieux d'être ou de
vivre,
Et pourquoi le Seigneur, qui seul lit à son livre,
Mêle éternellement dans un fatal hymen
Le chant de la nature au cri du genre humain?

As two cross currents 'neath a stream you see —
One from the seas, triumphant, blissful song!
Voice of the waves, which talked themselves
among;
The other, which from earth to heaven ran,
Was full of sorrow — the complaint of man;
And in this concert, singing night and day,
Each billow had its voice, each man his say.

And, as was said, vast ocean without cease,
Poured forth its voice of happiness and peace;
Songs, as the harps of Sion's temple raised,
The loveliness of all creation praised;
Its sound, borne by the swift-winged winds along,
For ever rose to God — a triumph song:
And all the waves which God alone can tame,
One ending — others still the hymn proclaim.
Like that great lion, whose awe-breathing guest
Was Daniel, oft the sea its roar supprest,
And when the sun sank flaming; to behold
God's hands, methought, passed 'neath its mane
of gold.

Yet piercing through this glorious symphony,
The other voice, like a scared courser's cry,
Like rusty hinge of Hell's gate, grating, sharp,
Or like a brazen bow on iron harp,
Grinding tears, cries, abuse, and venomed spite,
And fierce denial of each Christian rite,
And maledictions, clamours, blasphemies,
In the tumultuous waves of human cries,
Passed, as at eve in valleys meet the sight,
Flying in flocks, the sable birds of night.
What noise was this, whose echoes widely swept?
Alas! it was the earth and men who wept!

Friend! of these voices twain whose destiny,
Is ever to be born and ever die,
Whom hears th' Eternal, through eternity:
One — "Nature" said, and one — "Humanity."

Thus mused I! for my faithful soul had ne'er,
Alas! with bolder pinion cleaved the air; —
Ne'er through my gloom a brighter day had shone.
Long time I dreamed, revolving, one by one,
The abyss, the sea, hid from me, and beside
Th' abyss that in my soul was opened wide.
And much I questioned, why are we here? —
The end
Why? whither, after all, all this can tend?
What boots the soul? if best to die, or live?
Why God, who in His book alone can dive,
Joins in the fatal hymn since earth began,
The song of Nature, and the cries of Man?

INSTRUMENTATION

2 Flutes

Piccolo

2 Oboes

2 Clarinets (B-flat)

Bass Clarinet (B-flat)

2 Bassoons

4 Horns (E-flat)

3 Trumpets (E-flat)

3 Trombones

Tuba

Timpani

Percussion
(Tam-Tam, Bass Dum, Cymbals)

Harp

Violins I

Violins II

Violas

Violoncellos

Basses

Duration: ca. 38 minutes

First Performance: January 7, 1857
Weimar: Hofkapelle Weimar
Franz Liszt, conductor

ISBN: 978-1-60874-021-5

This score is an unabridged reprint of the score
first issued in Leipzig by Breitkopf & Härtel, 1908. Plate F. L. 2

Printed in the USA
First Printing: August, 2011

CE QU'ON ENTEND SUR LA MONTAGNE

Symphonic Poem No. 1

S. 95

FRANZ LISZT (1811-1886)

Piccolo Flöte.
2 Flöten.
2 Hoboen.
2 Klarinetten in B.
Bassklarinette in B.
2 Fagotte.
1. u. 2. Horn in Es.
3. u. 4. Horn in Es.
1. u. 2. Trompete in Es.
3. Trompete in Es.
2 Tenorposaunen.
Bassposaune u. Tuba.
Pauken in Fis. B. Es.
Tamtam.
Becken.
Grosse Trommel.
(mit gewöhnlichen Paukenschlägeln)
Harfe.
1. Violinen.
2. Violinen.
Bratschen.
Violoncelle.
Kontrabässe.

Poco Allegro.

con Sordino
pp misterioso e tranquillo

poco cresc. -

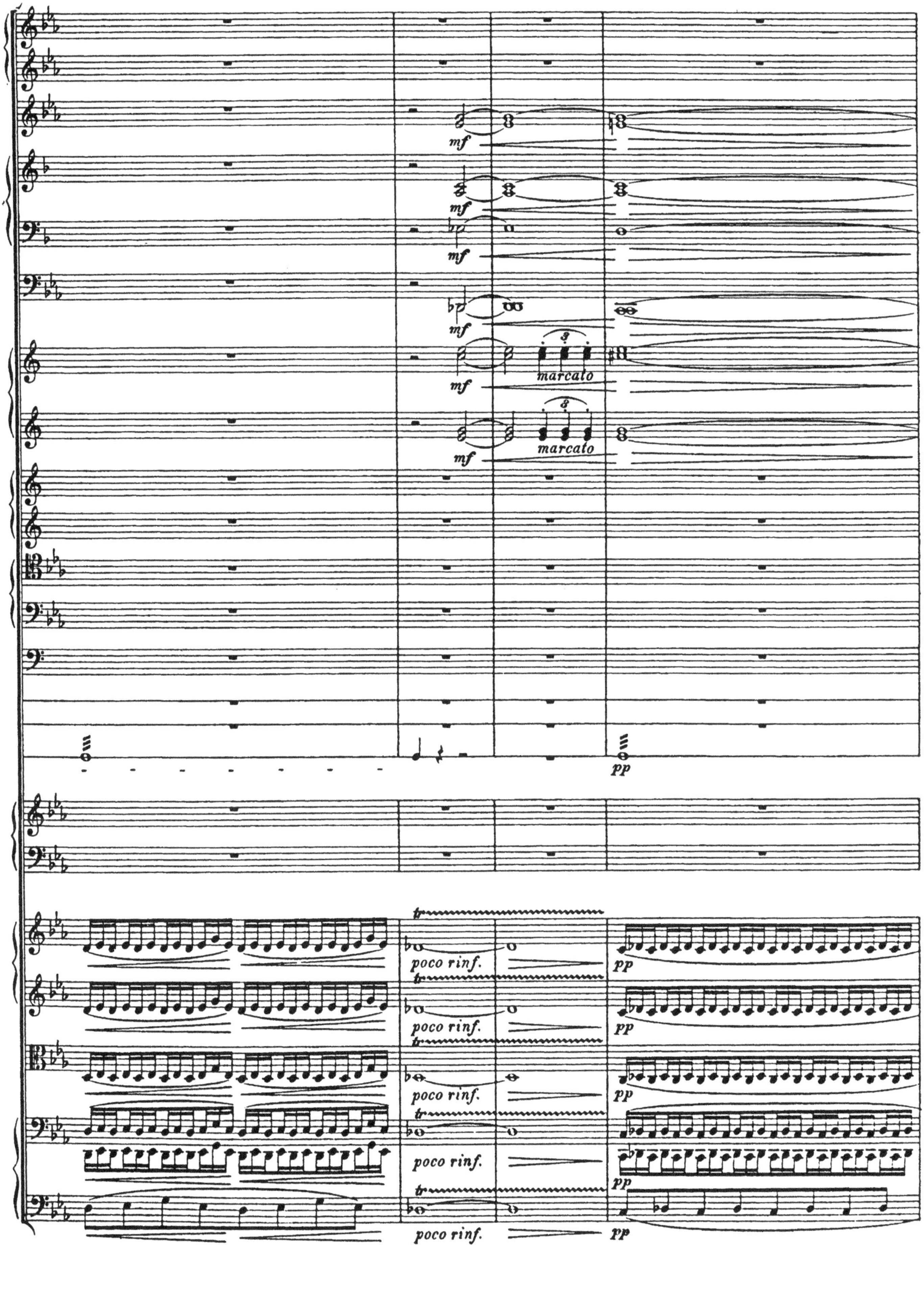
mf
marcato
tr
poco rinf.
pp

6

mf
mf
mf
mf
mf
marcato
mf
marcato
poco cresc.
tr
poco rinf.
tr
poco rinf.
tr
poco rinf.
tr
poco rinf.
tr
poco rinf.

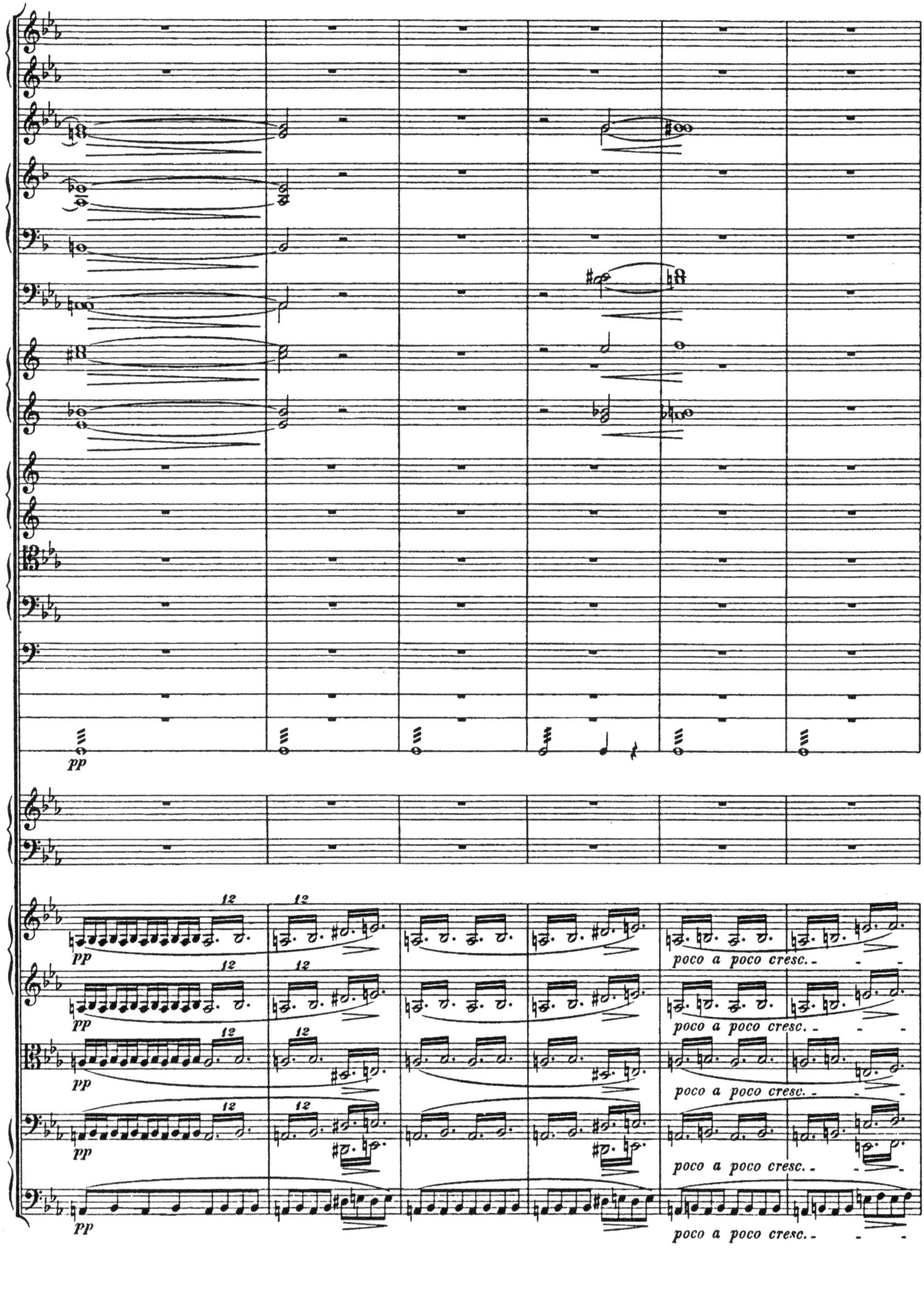
pp
12
poco a poco cresc.

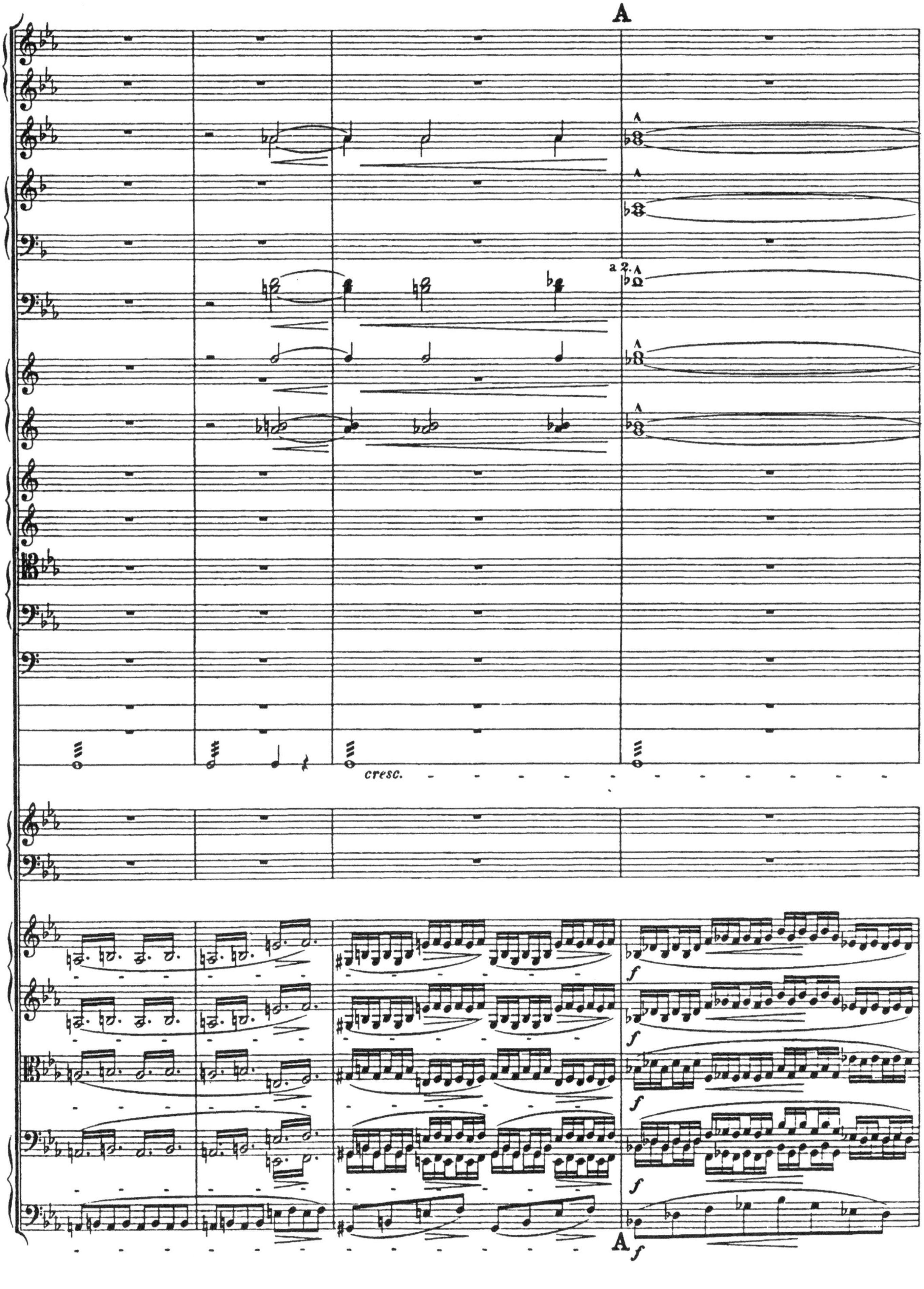
A
a 2.
cresc.
f
f
f
f
A
f

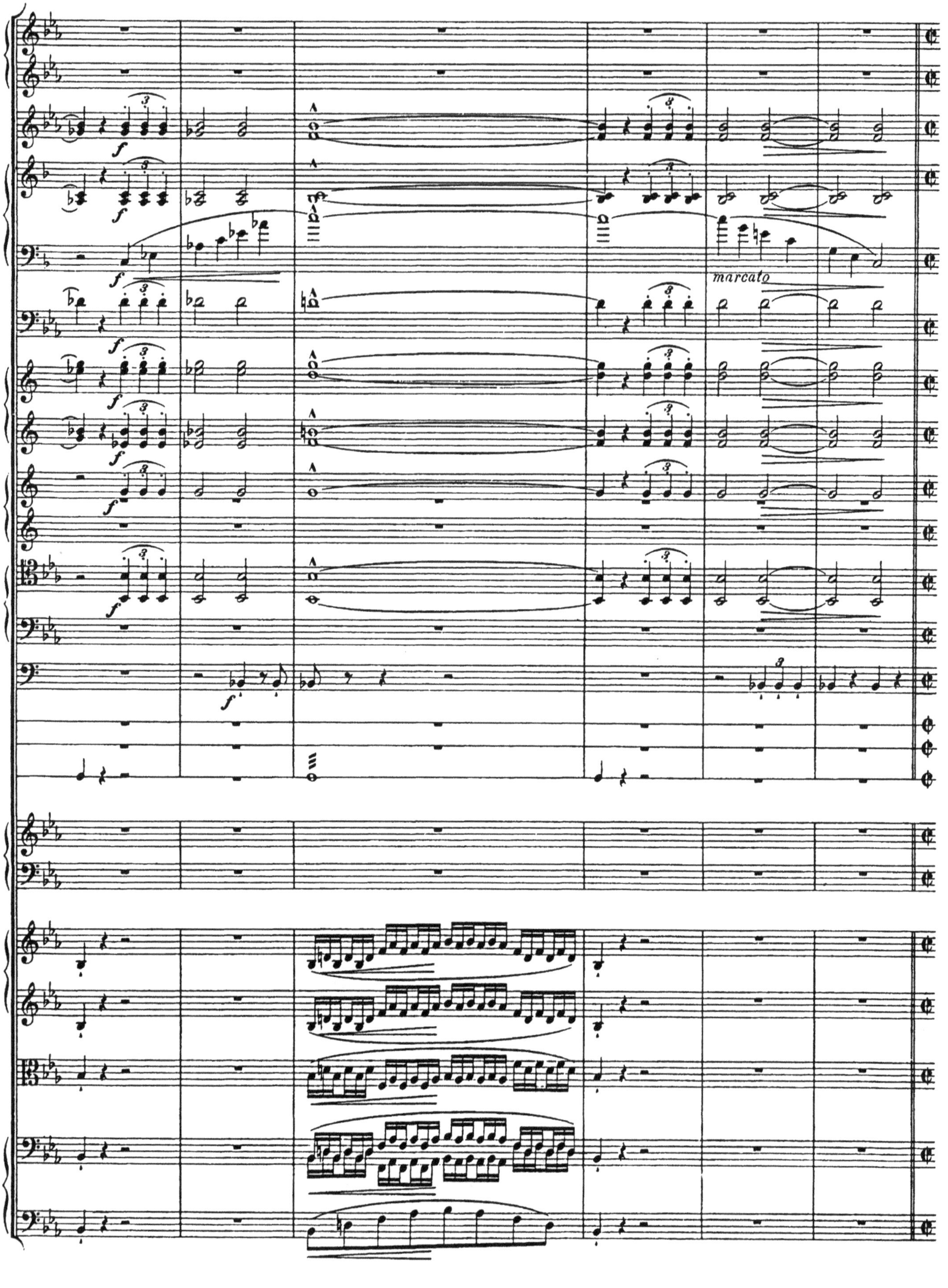
marcato

Poco a poco più di moto sin' al Allegro mosso.

Muta B in Gis, Es in Cis.

Poco a poco più di moto sin' al Allegro mosso.

dolce grazioso
p
marcato
p
marcato
trem.
sempre p
trem.
sempre p

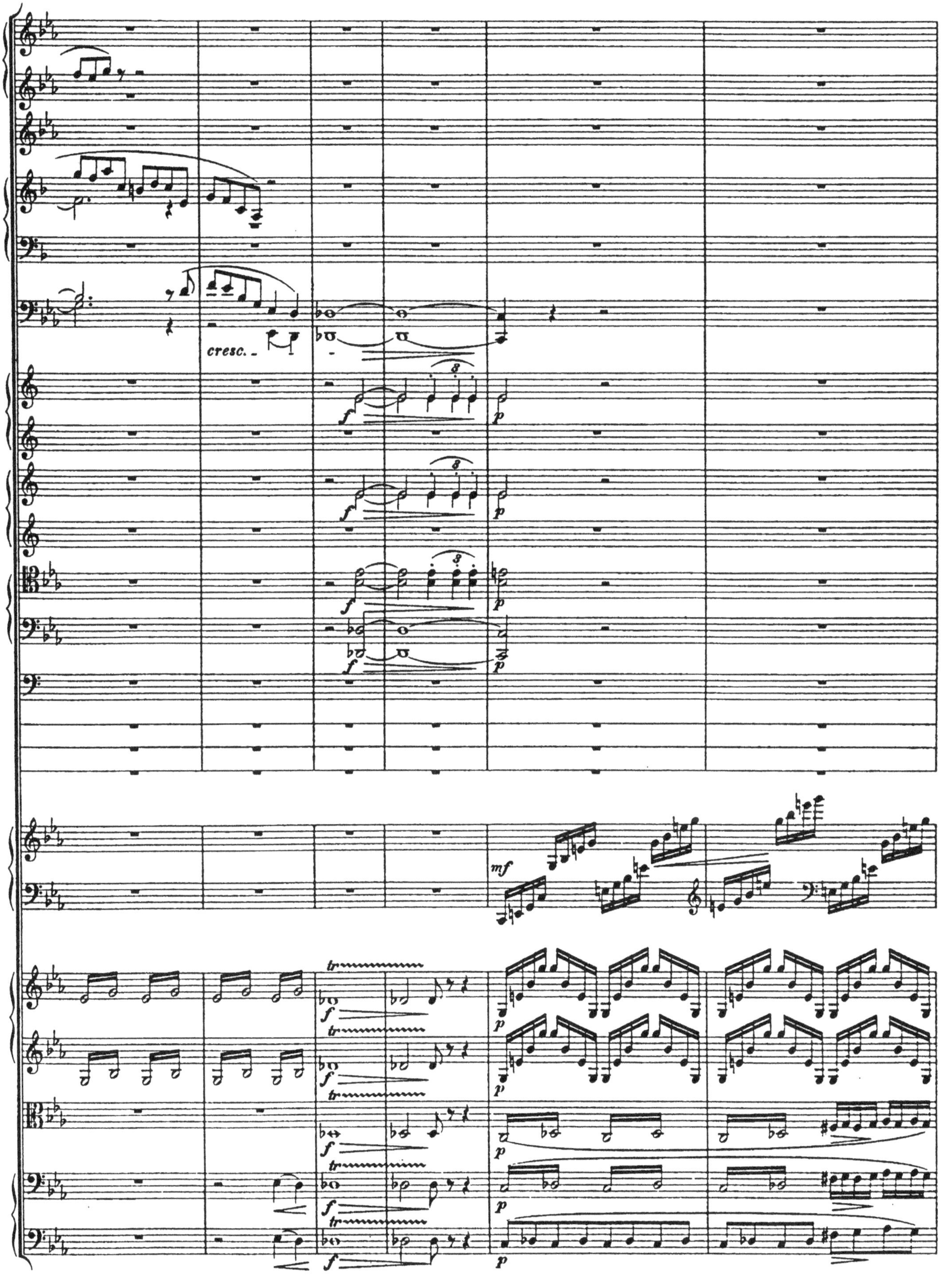
cresc.
tr
mf

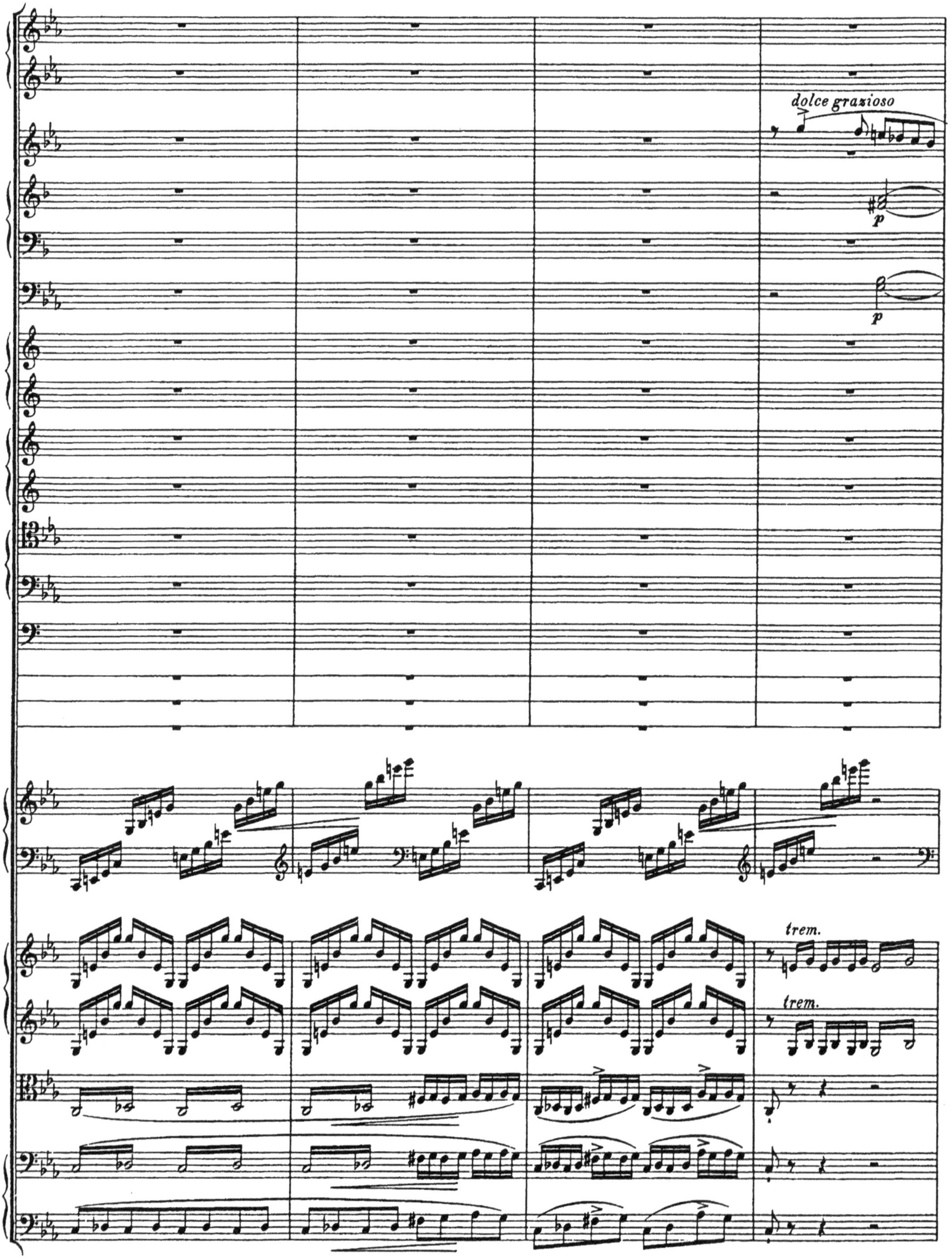
dolce grazioso
p
p
trem.
trem.

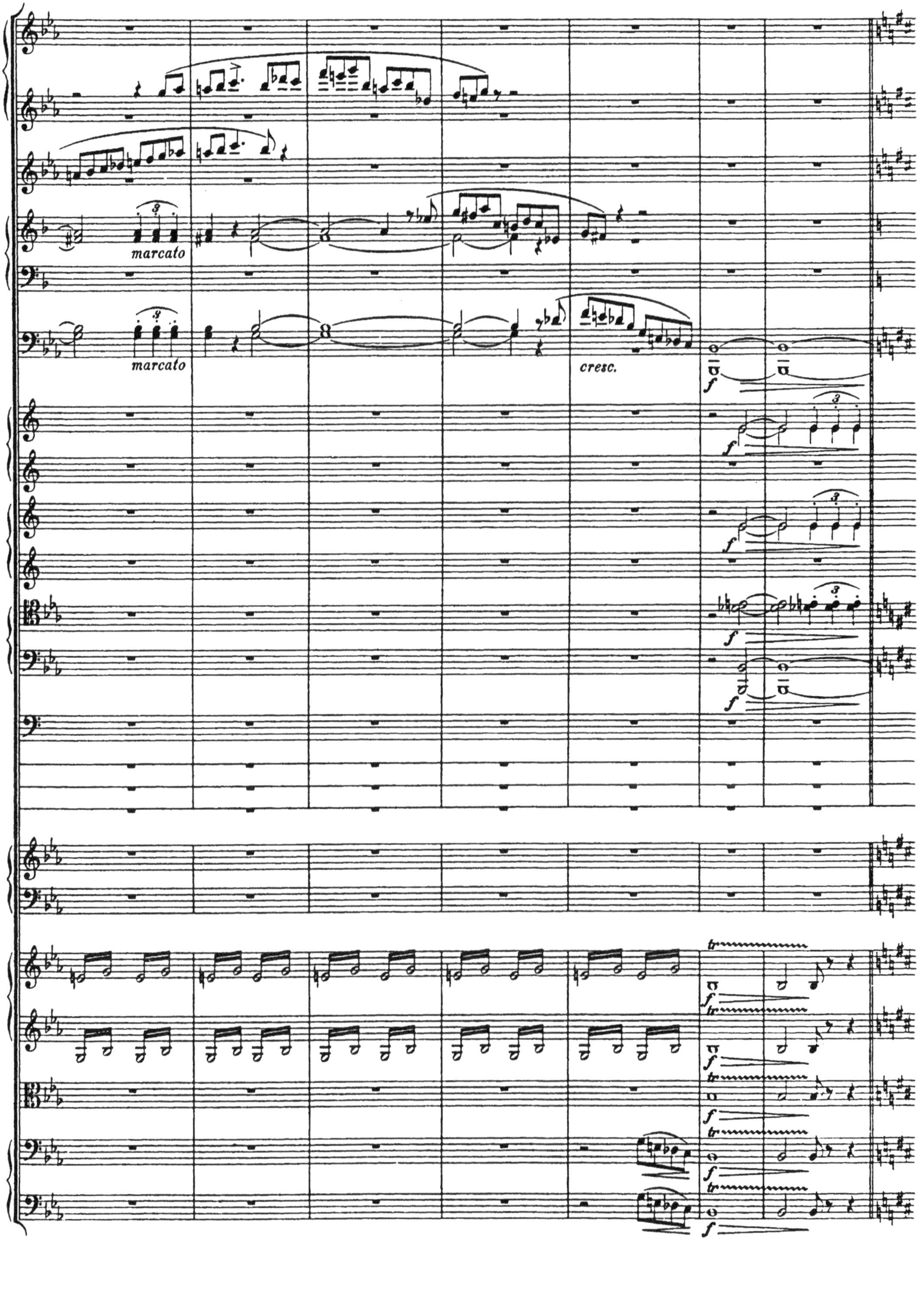
marcato
marcato
cresc.

B Allegro mosso.
p
un poco marcato
un poco marcato
p
p
p
p
p
p
pizz.
p
pizz.
p
B Allegro mosso.

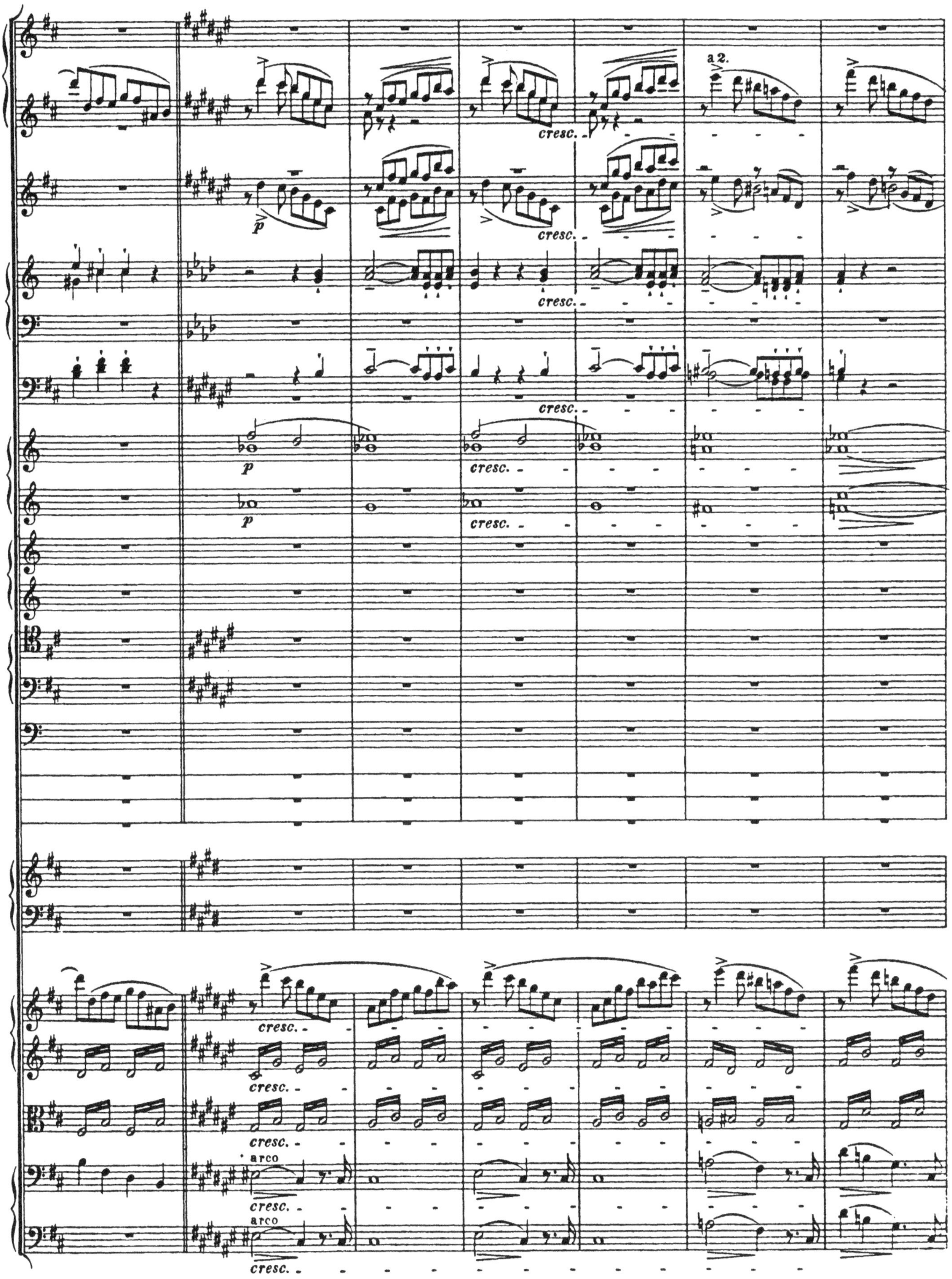
a 2.
cresc.
p
arco

18

C
p marcato
p marcato
p marcato
p
p
p
in Fis. Gis. Cis.
Mit Pauken-
schlägeln.
pp
p
p
p
p
p
p
C

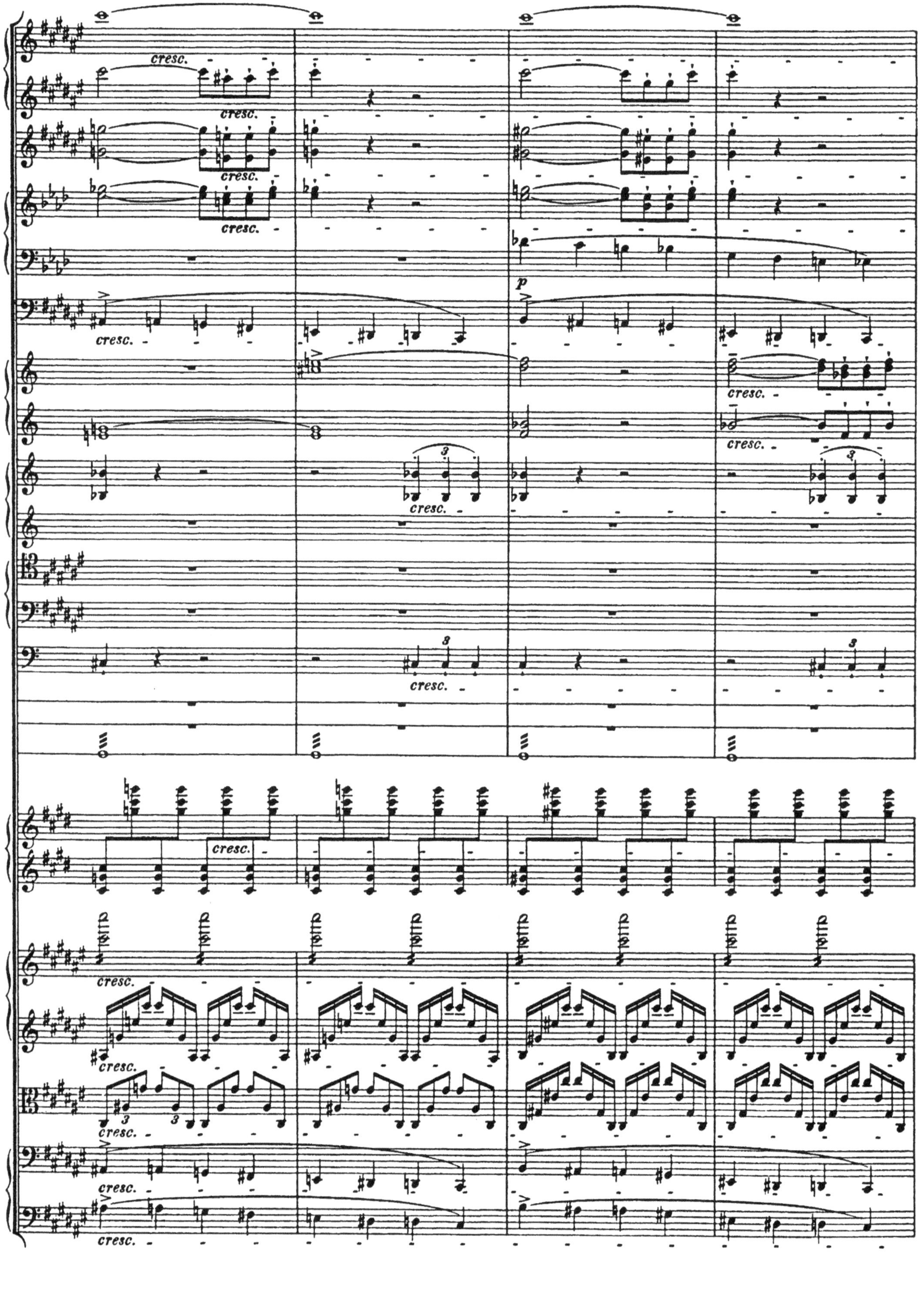
cresc.
p
3
cresc.

lange Pause.
lunga Pausa.
a 2.
cresc.
molto
rinf. molto
a 2.
poco cresc.
lange Pause.
lunga Pausa.
molto
lange Pause.
lunga Pausa.
rinf. molto
rinf. molto
lange Pause.
lunga Pausa.

Maestoso assai.

Maestoso assai.

NB. Das erste Achtel der Figur [figure] ist nicht als Sechzehntel [figure] sondern überall als Achtel zu accentuieren.
The first quaver of the figure [figure] *must be accented throughout not as a semiquaver* [figure] *, but as a quaver.*
La première croche de la figure [figure] sera partout accentuée non comme double croche [figure] mais bien comme croche.

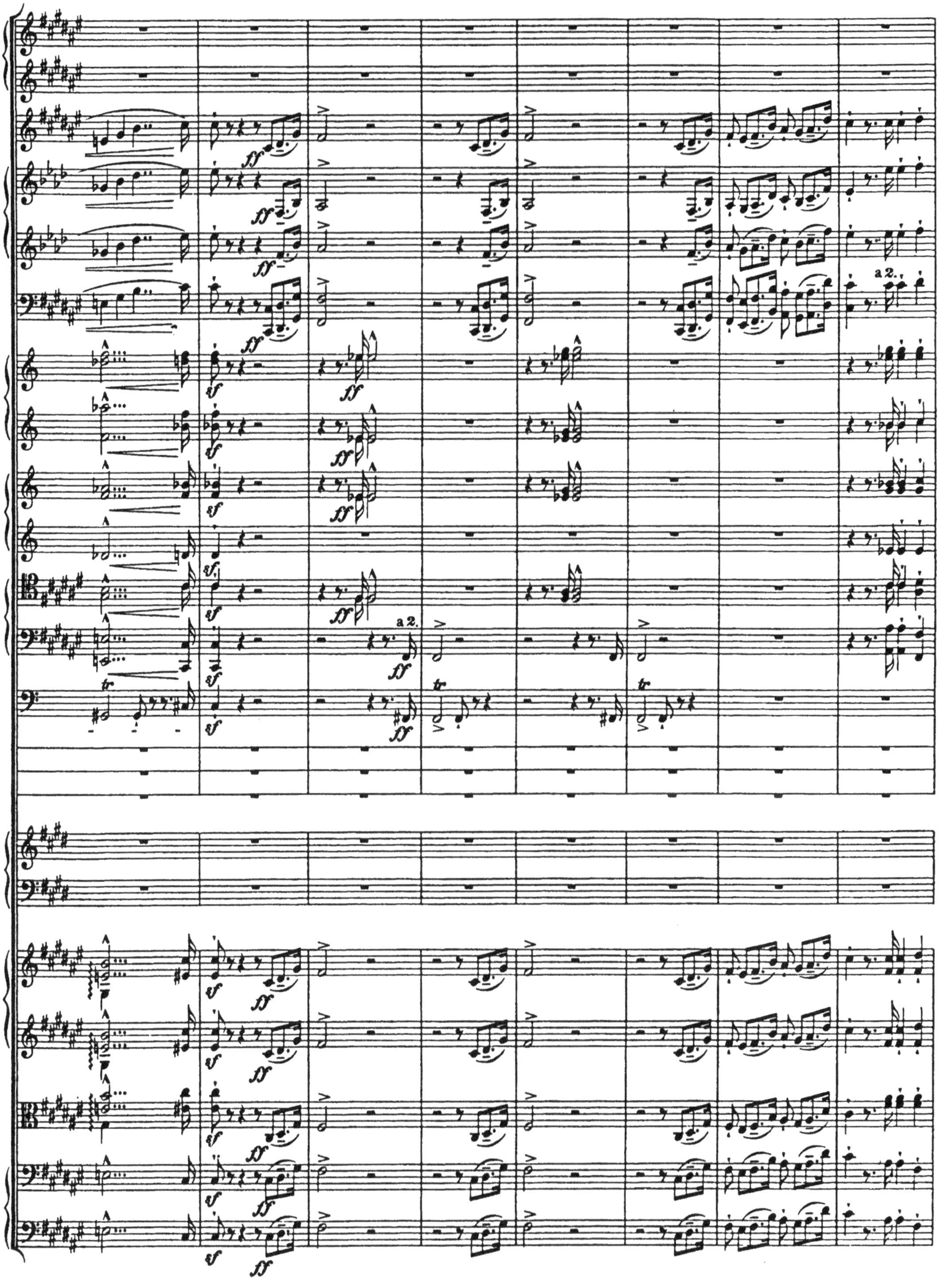

a 2.
ff
sf
tr

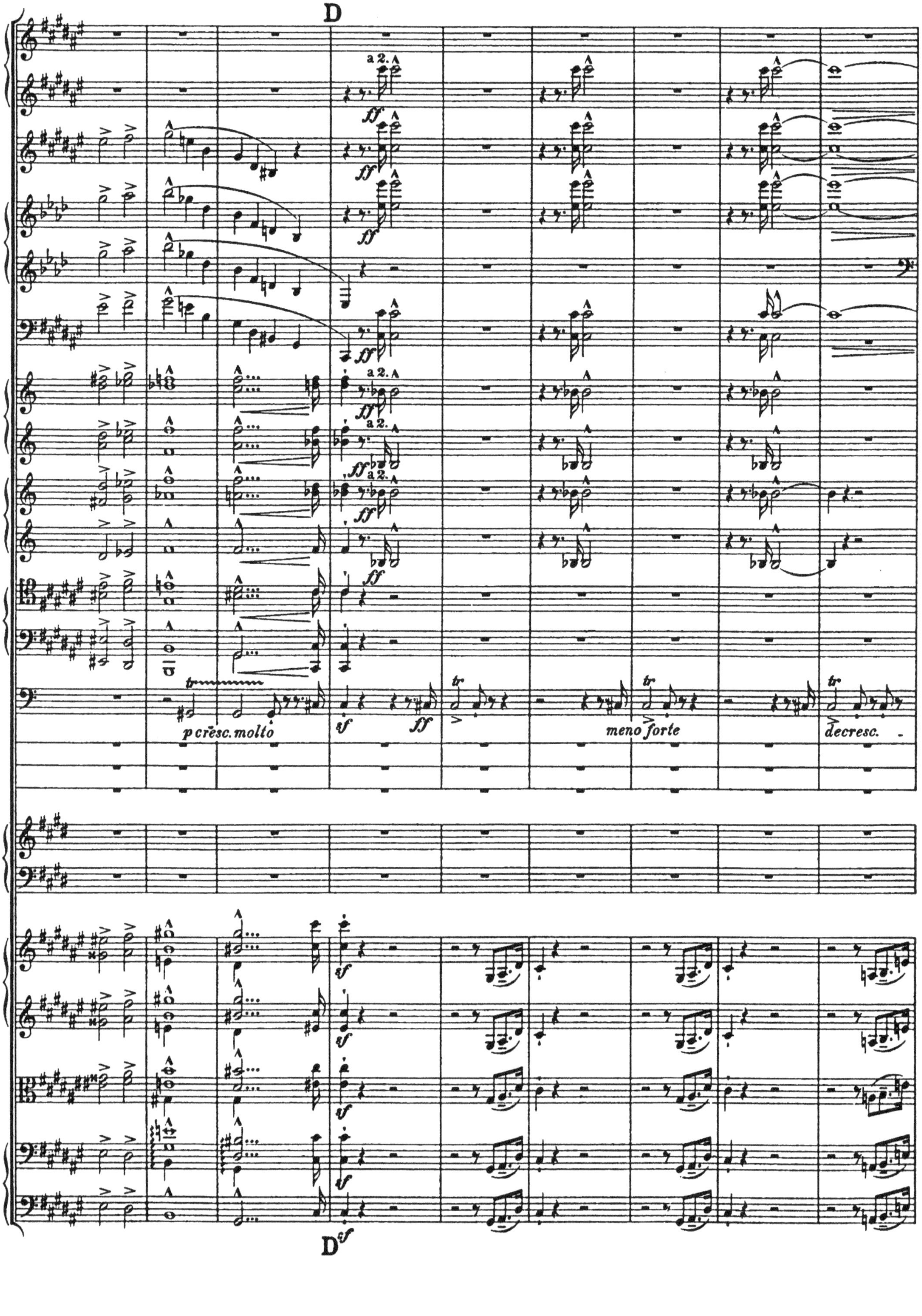
D
a 2.
ff
p cresc. molto
sf
meno forte
decresc.
D
sf

dim.
dim.
dim.
dim.
ff
ff
ff
tr
ff
meno forte
decresc.
dim.
dim.
dim.
dim.
dim.

Alla breve.

Muta Gis in B, Cis in H.

Vcll.

div.

Alla breve.

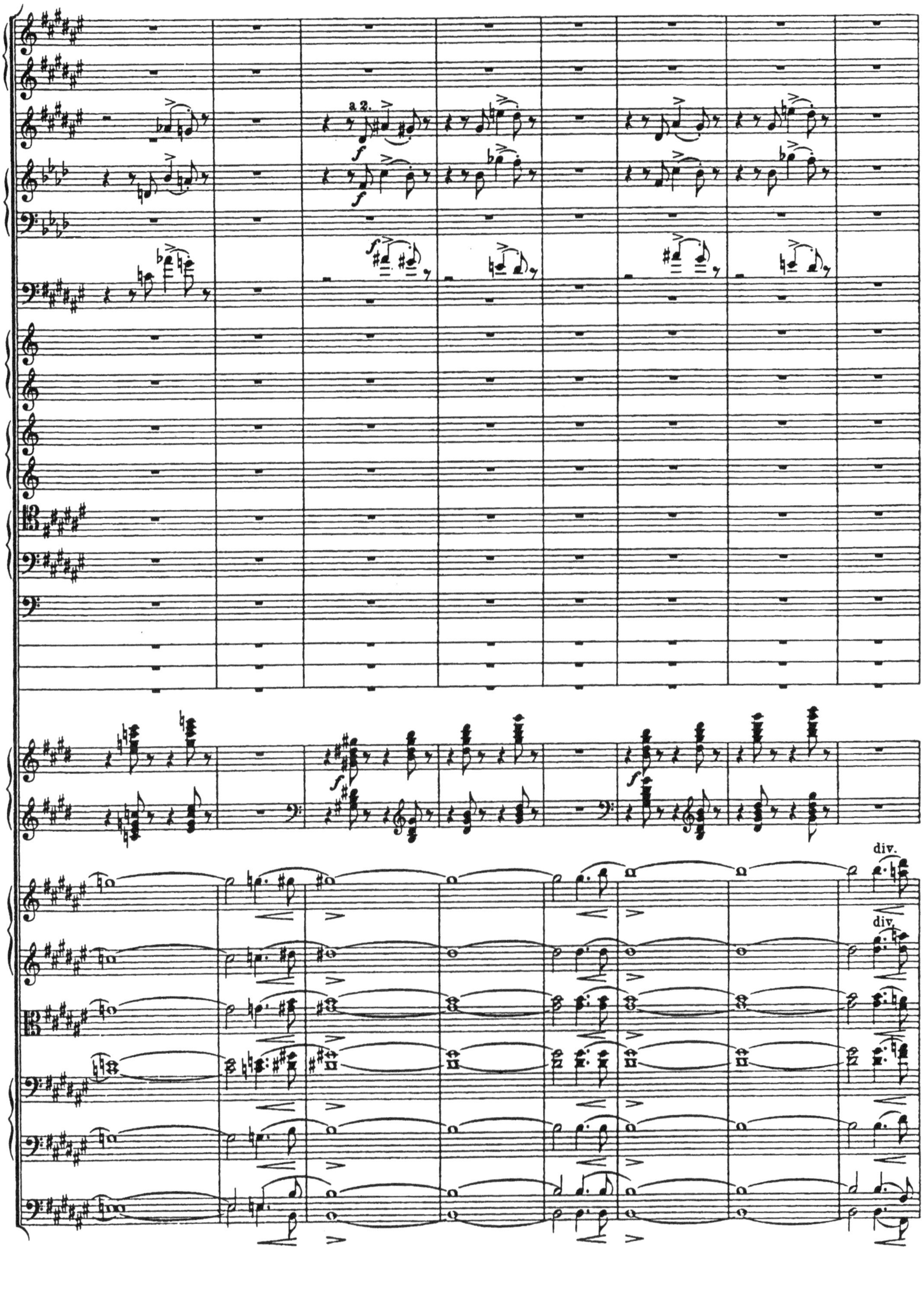
a 2.
f
div.
div.

E
accelerando
a 2.
f accentuato
f accentuato
a 2.
f
a 2.
f
a 2.
f
in Fis. B. H.
p
p
cresc.
pp
pp
pp
cresc.
cresc.
cresc.
unis.
ff impetuoso
accelerando
E

Allegro con moto.

Allegro con moto.

F

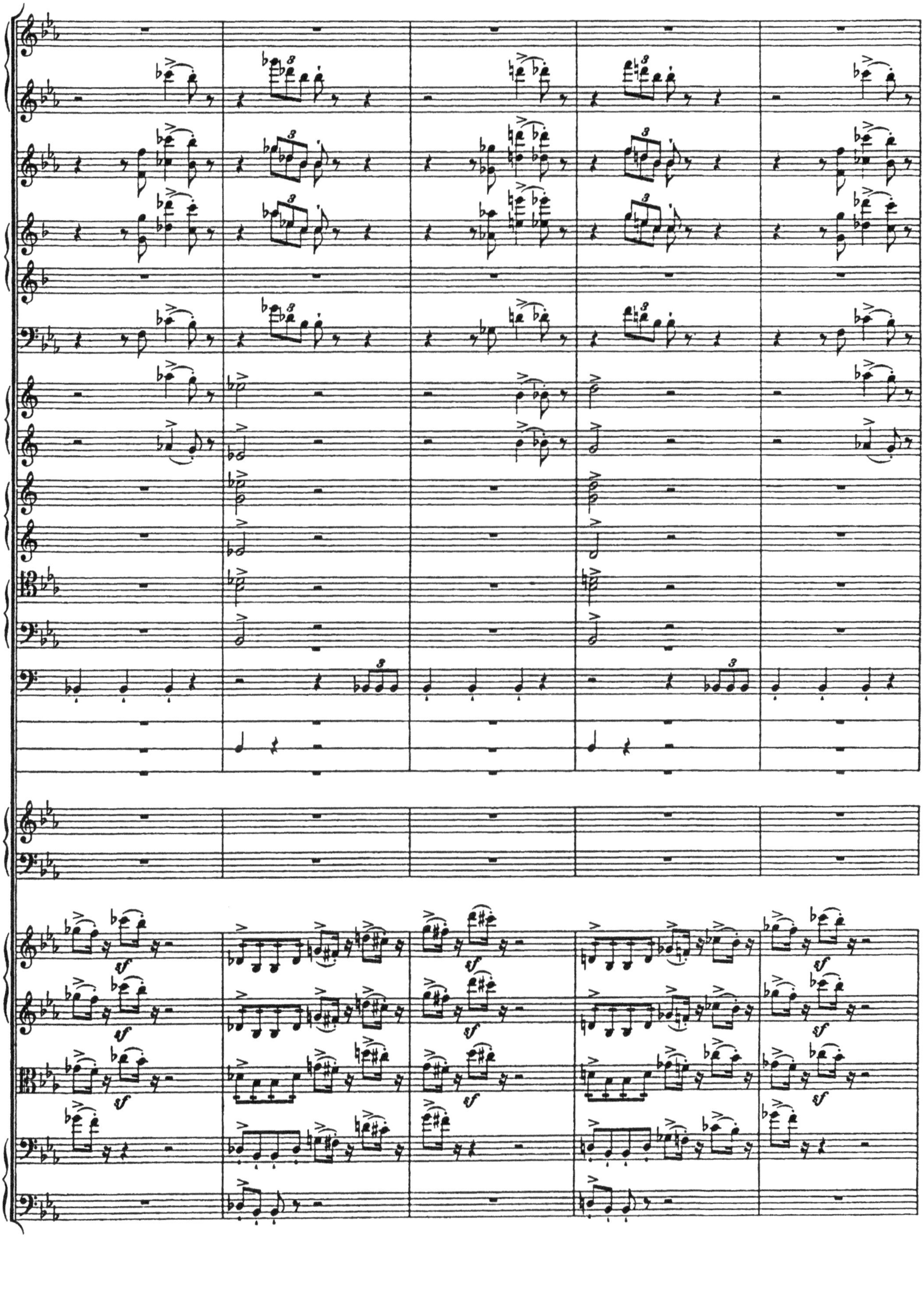

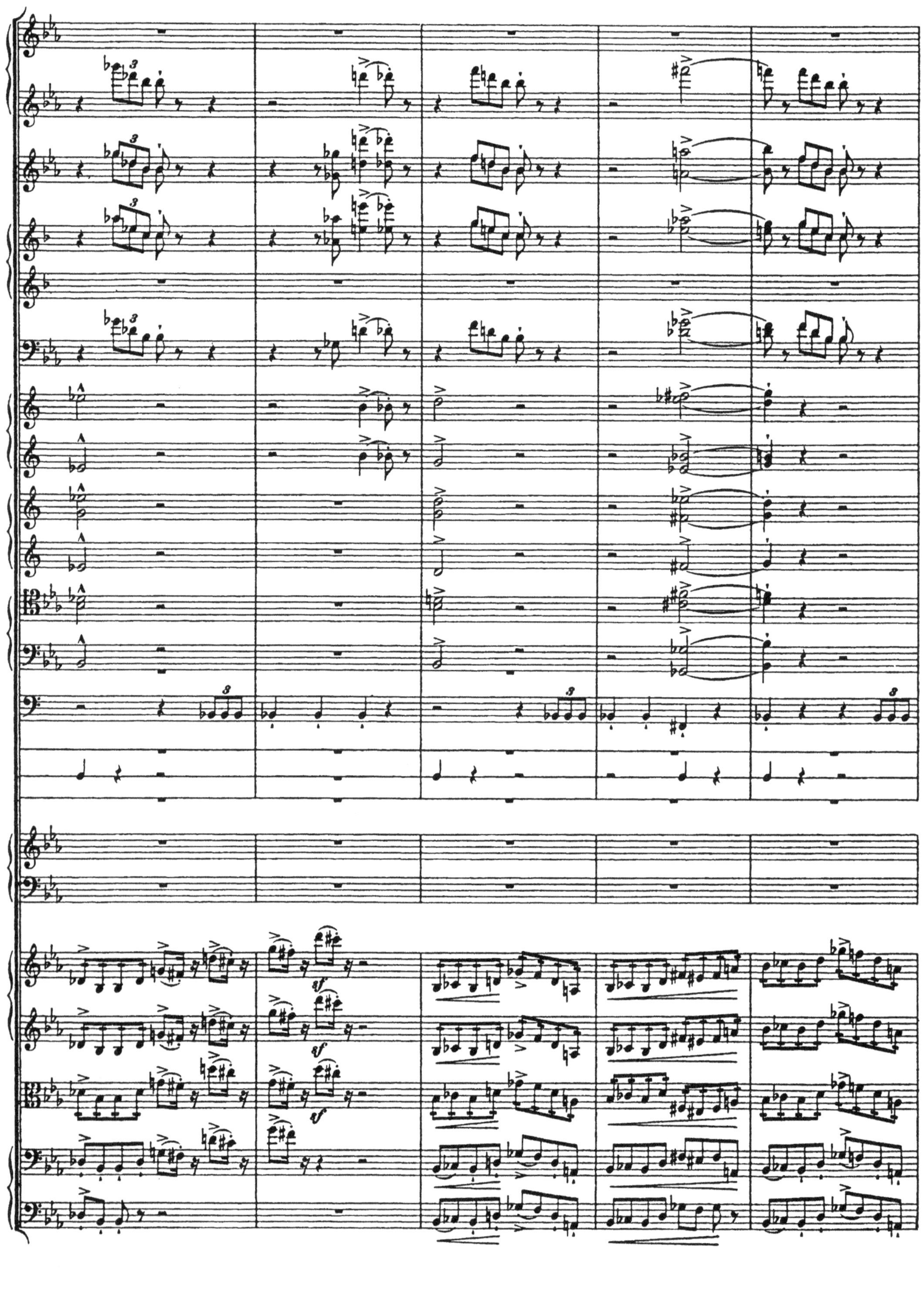
sf
sf
sf

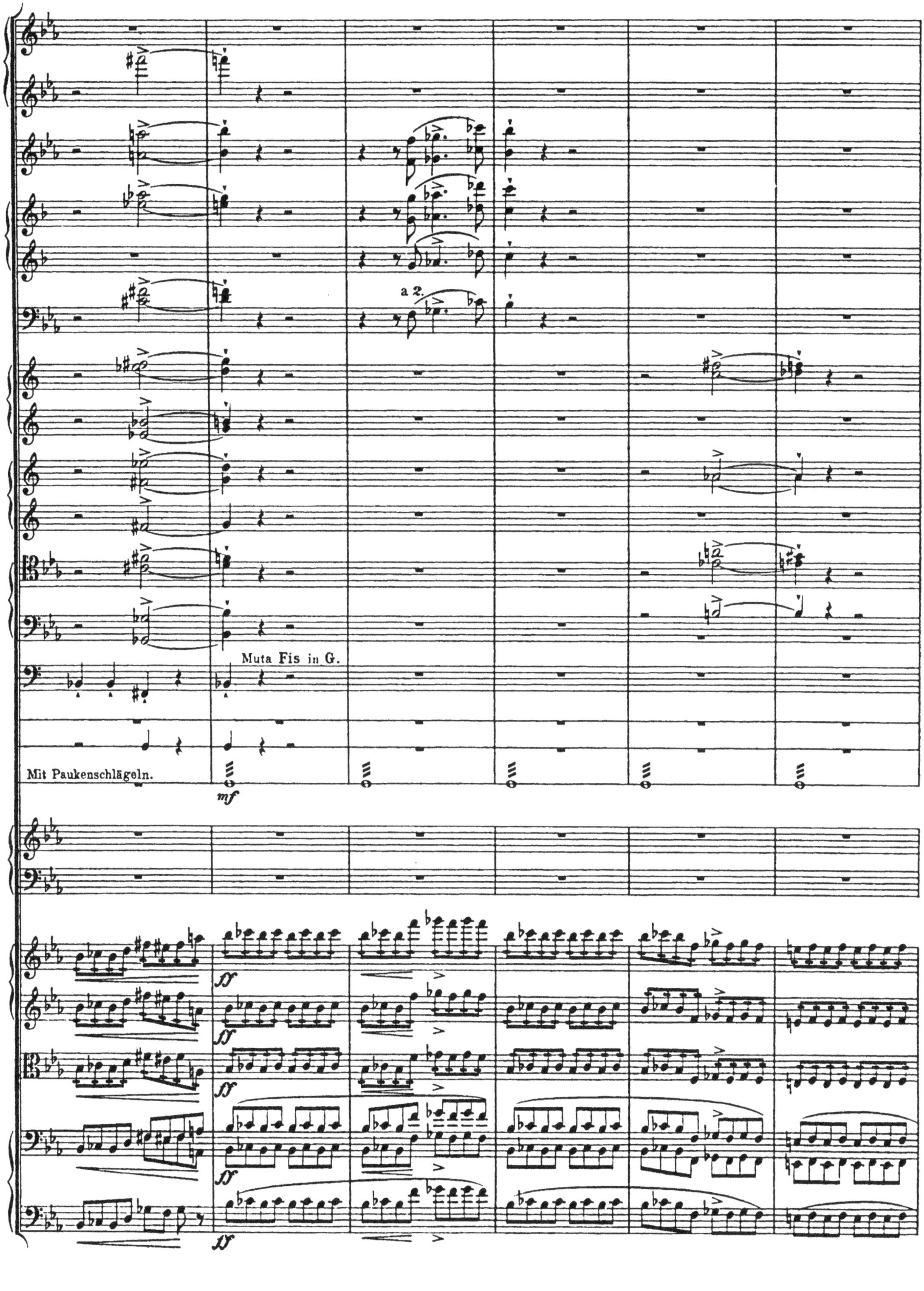
a 2.
Muta Fis in G.
Mit Paukenschlägeln.

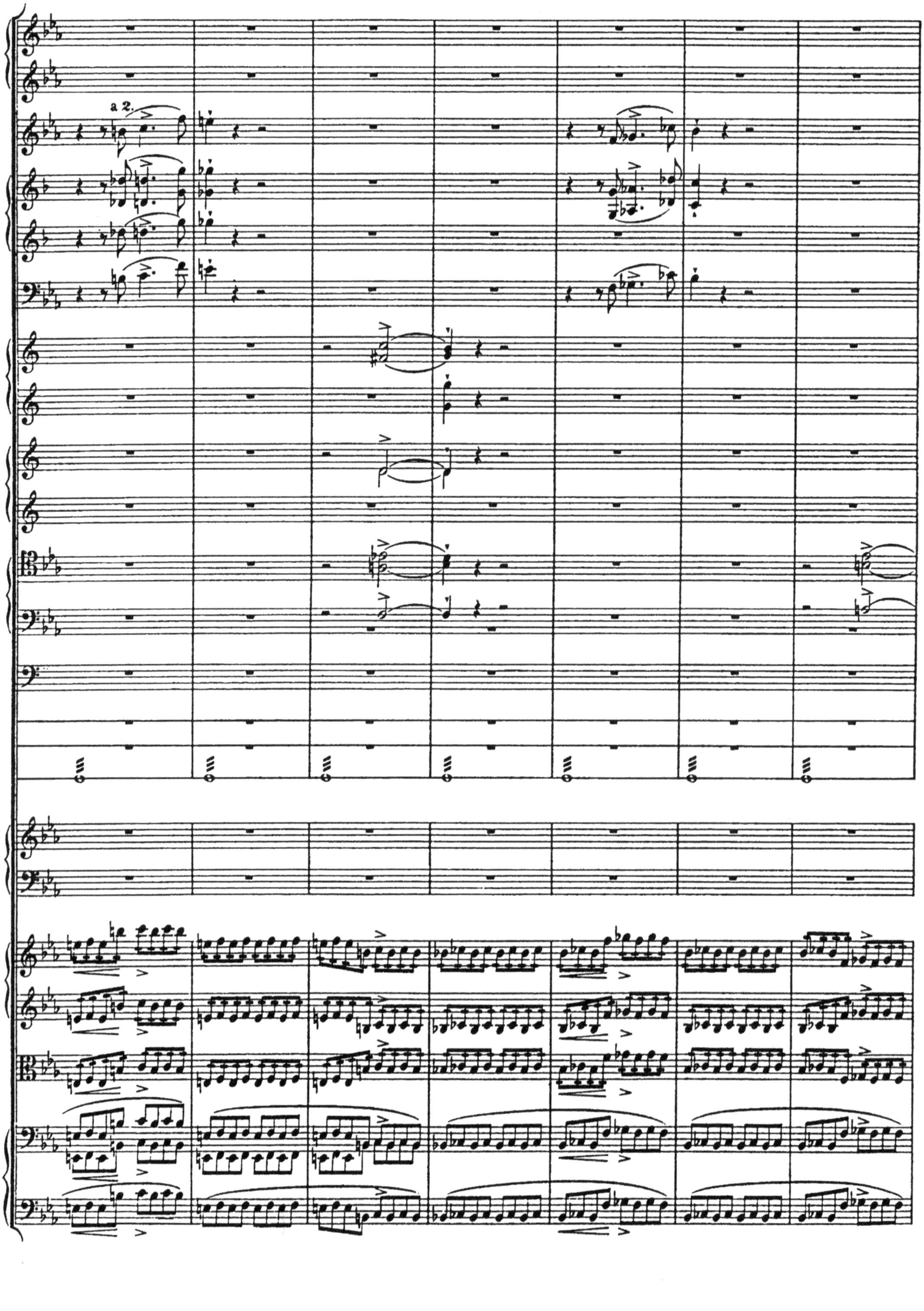
a 2.

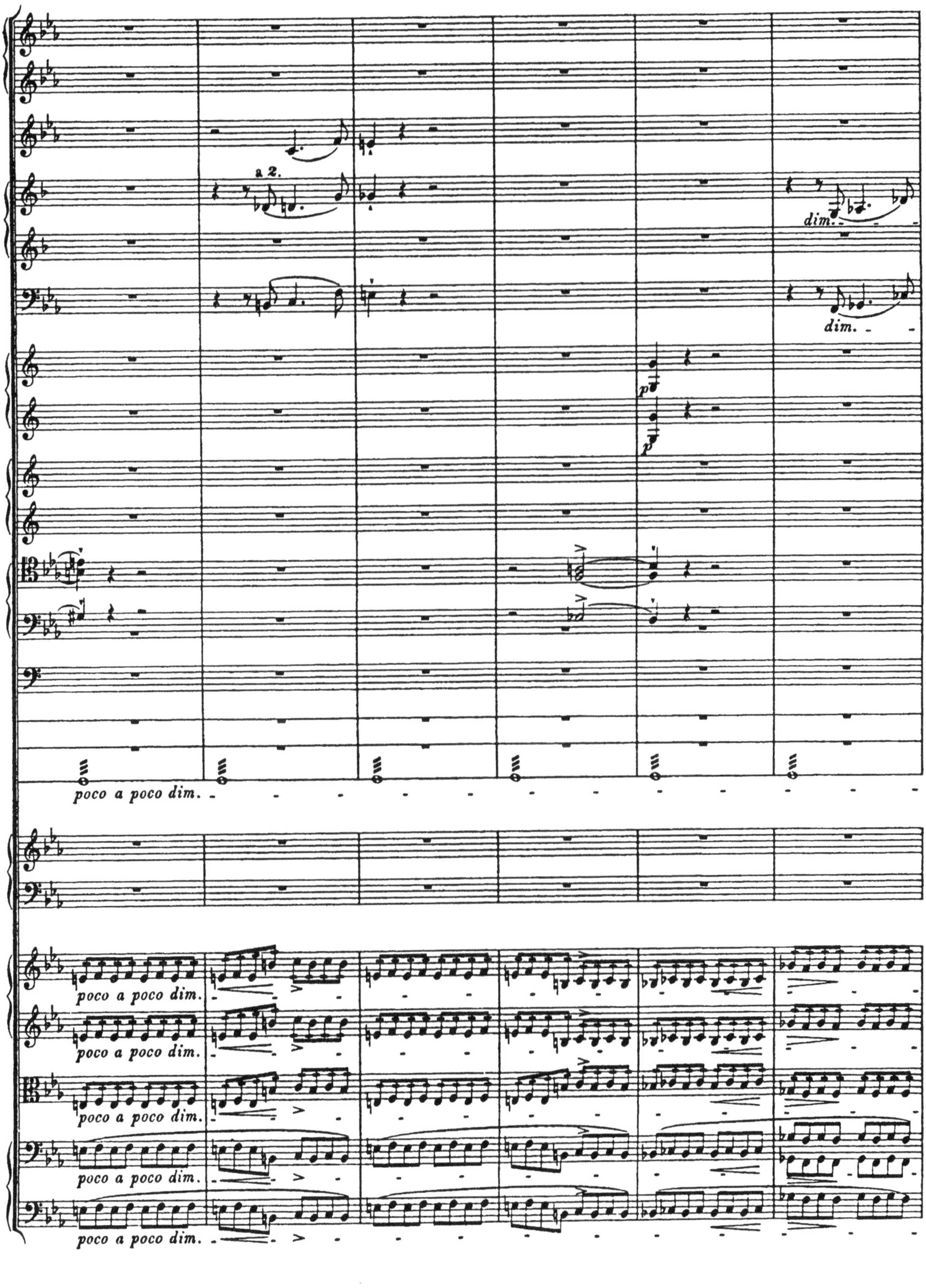

36

Der Buchstabe R.... bedeutet ein geringes Ritardando, so zu sagen: ein leises crescendo des Rhythmus.
The letter R.... signifies a slight Ritardando, so to speak: a gentle crescendo of the rhythm.
La lettre R.... signifie un petit Ritardando, c'est-à-dire: un doux crescendo du rhythme.

Allegro mestoso. sempre Alla breve.

Allegro mestoso. sempre Alla breve.

*) Die Tamtamschläge leise, aber vibrierend.
The strokes on the gong soft, but vibrating.
Les coups de tam-tam légers, mais vibrants.

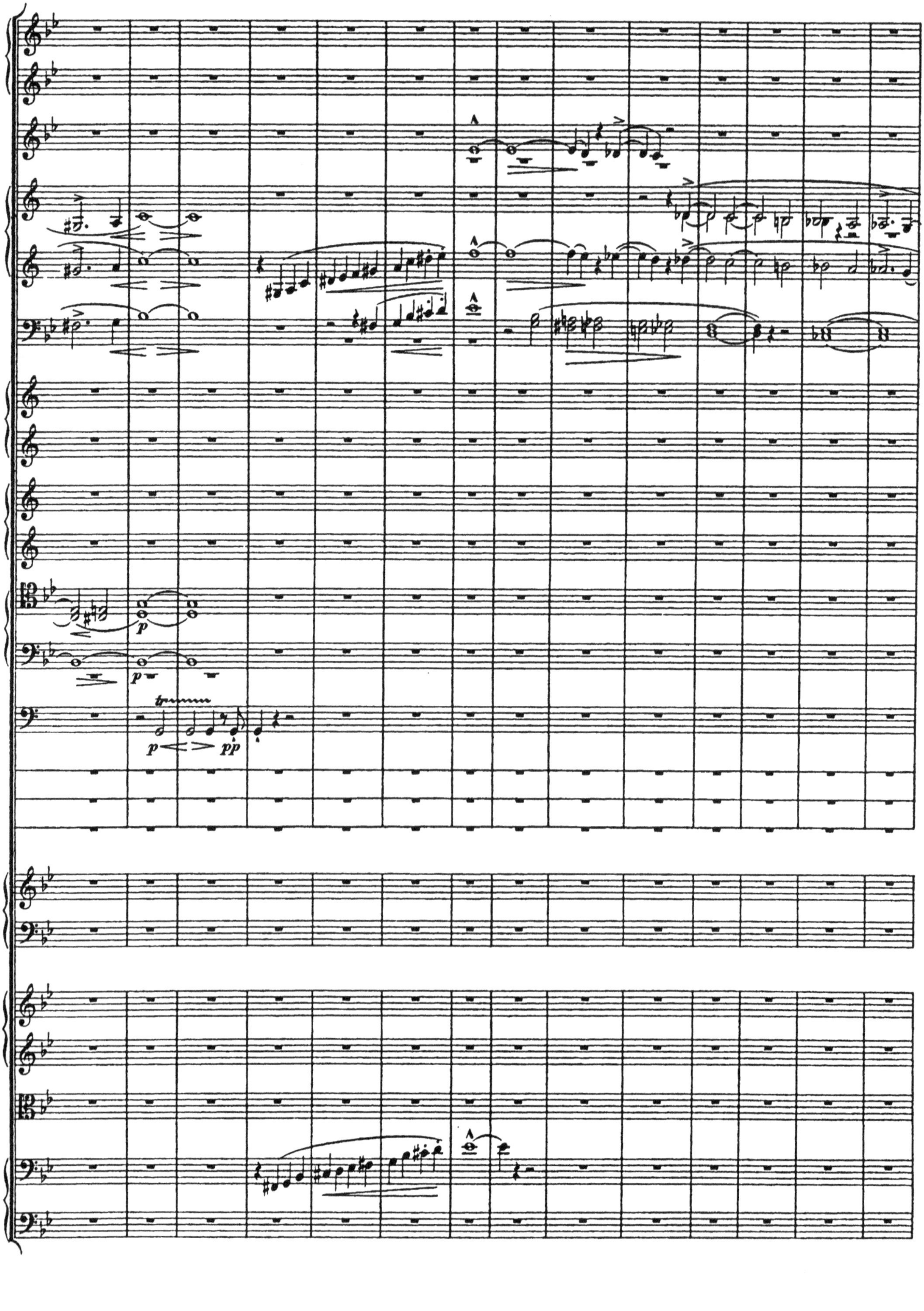
tr
p
pp

H
R.
gestopft
p
gestopft
div.
arco
p
mf tranquillo
dim.
perdendo
pizz.
arco
pp tranquillo
dim.
perdendo
pizz.
H
R.

pp dolce, tranquillo molto
smorz.
pp dolce, tranquillo molto
smorz.
pp dolce, tranquillo molto
smorz.
pp
smorz.
Solo
arco
dolce, tranquillo molto
tr
sempre dolcissimo

I
a 2.
mf dolente
a 2.
mf dolente
dolente
dolente
p
dolente
p
p lugubre
ppp
lang
lunga
perdendosi
e rallent
ppp
I

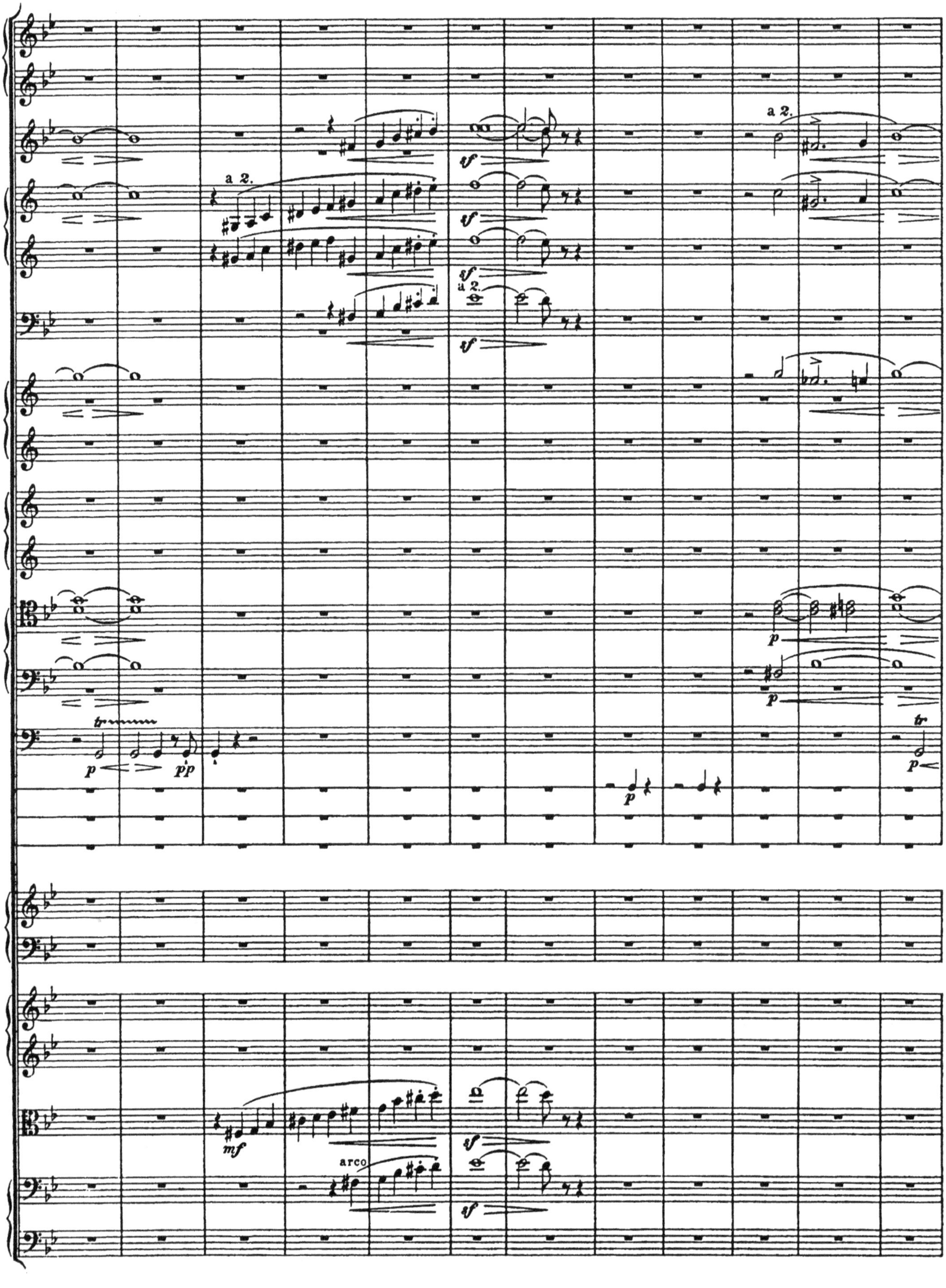
a 2.
sf
p
pp
mf
arco
tr

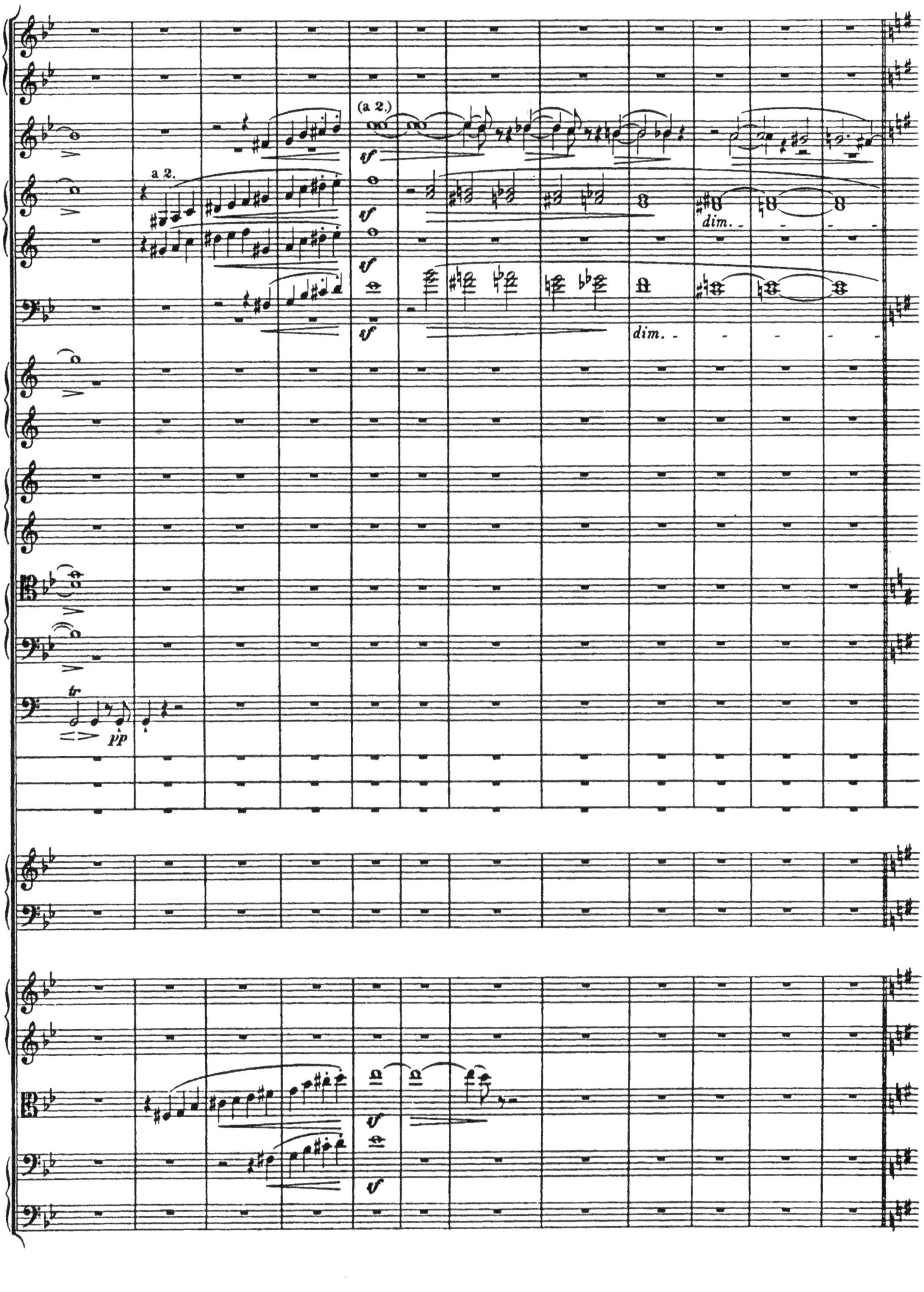
(a 2.)
a 2.
sf
dim.
tr
pp

J
(a 2.)
p
p
p
mf
dim.
div.
dolente
p tranquillo
arco
pp tranquillo
dim.
pizz.
dim.
pizz.
J

pp
smorz.
pp
smorz.
pp
smorz.
pp
smorz.
ppp
Solo
dolce, tranquillo molto

K
Allegro agitato assai.

K
Allegro agitato assai.

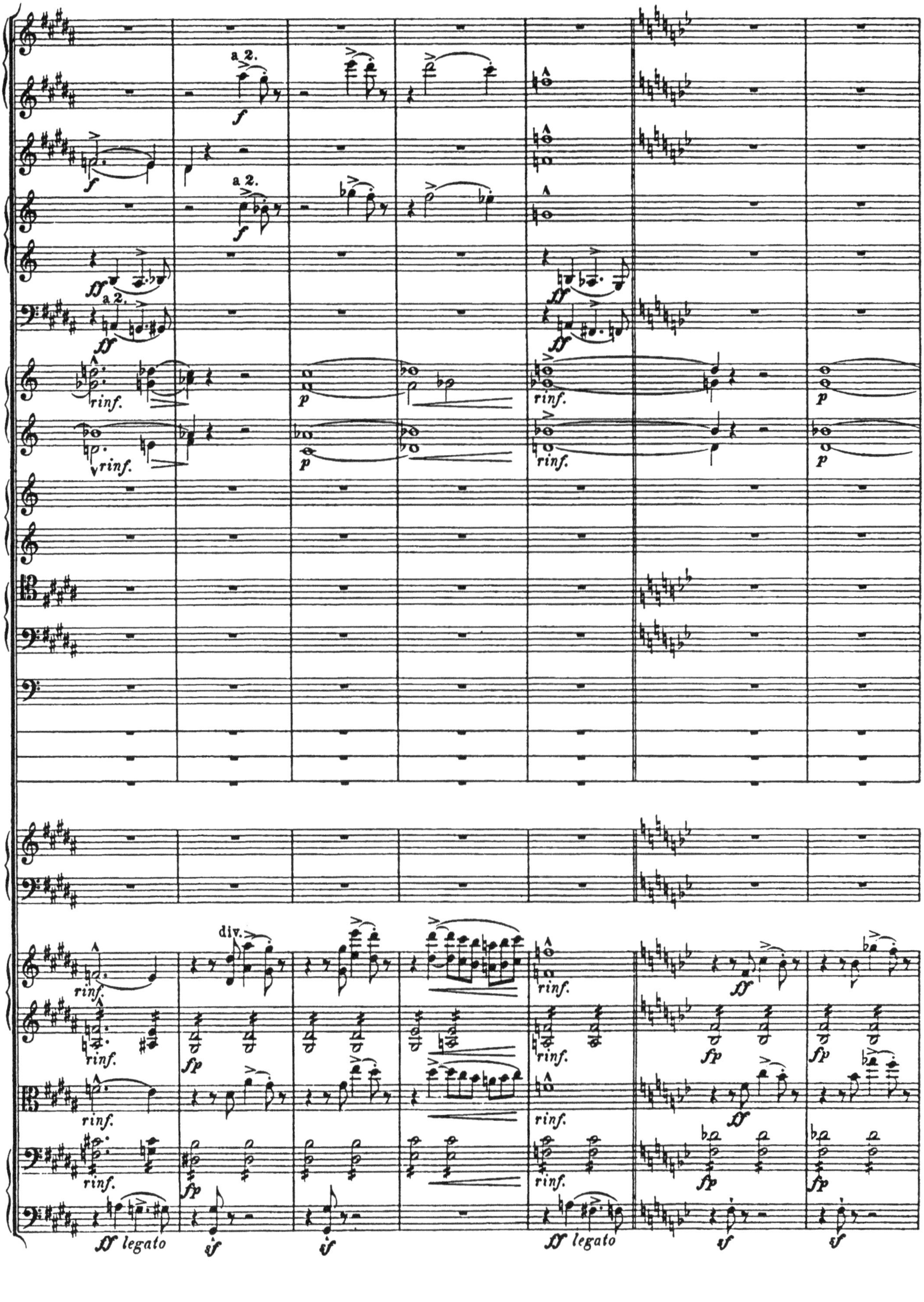
a 2.
f
rinf.
ff
p
div.
fp
ff legato
sf

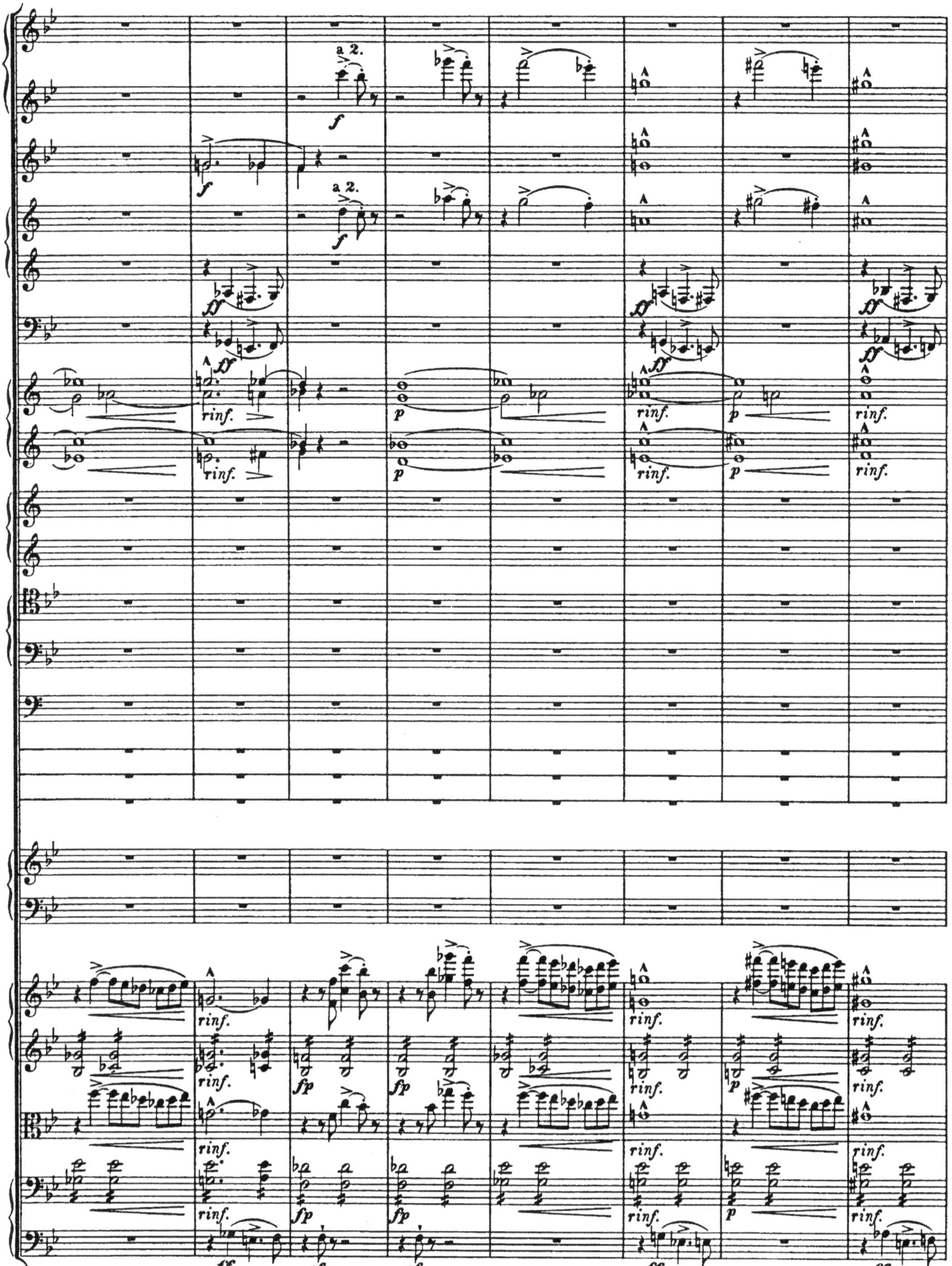
a 2.
f
a 2.
f
ff
rinf.
p
fp
sf

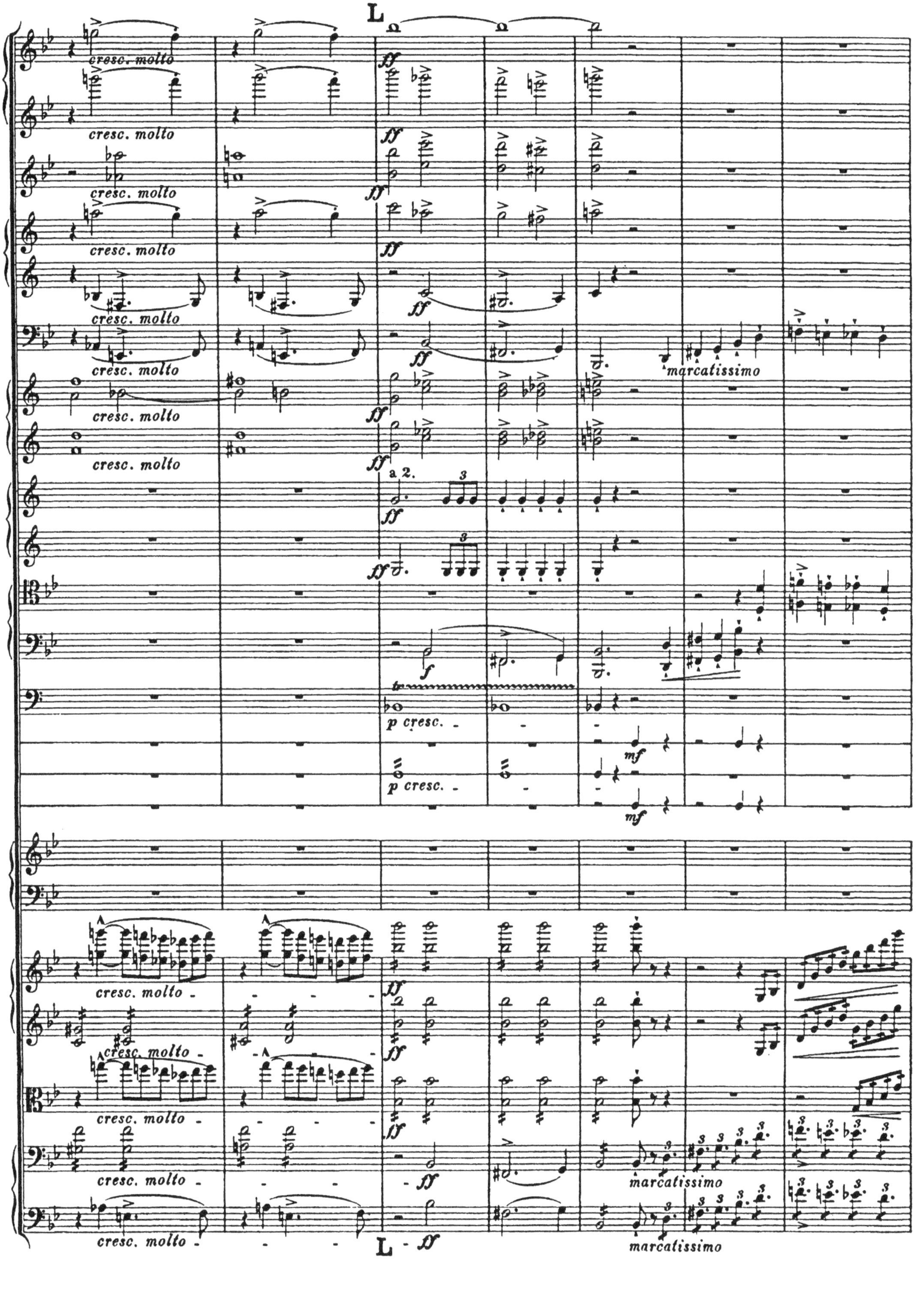
L
cresc. molto
ff
a 2.
f
p cresc.
mf
marcatissimo
L

marcatissimo
a 2.
p cresc.
p cresc
mf
ff
marcatissimo
marcatissimo

sempre ff
sempre ff
sempre ff
p cresc.
p cresc.
mf
mf
div.
sempre ff
sempre ff
sempre ff

M
accelerando

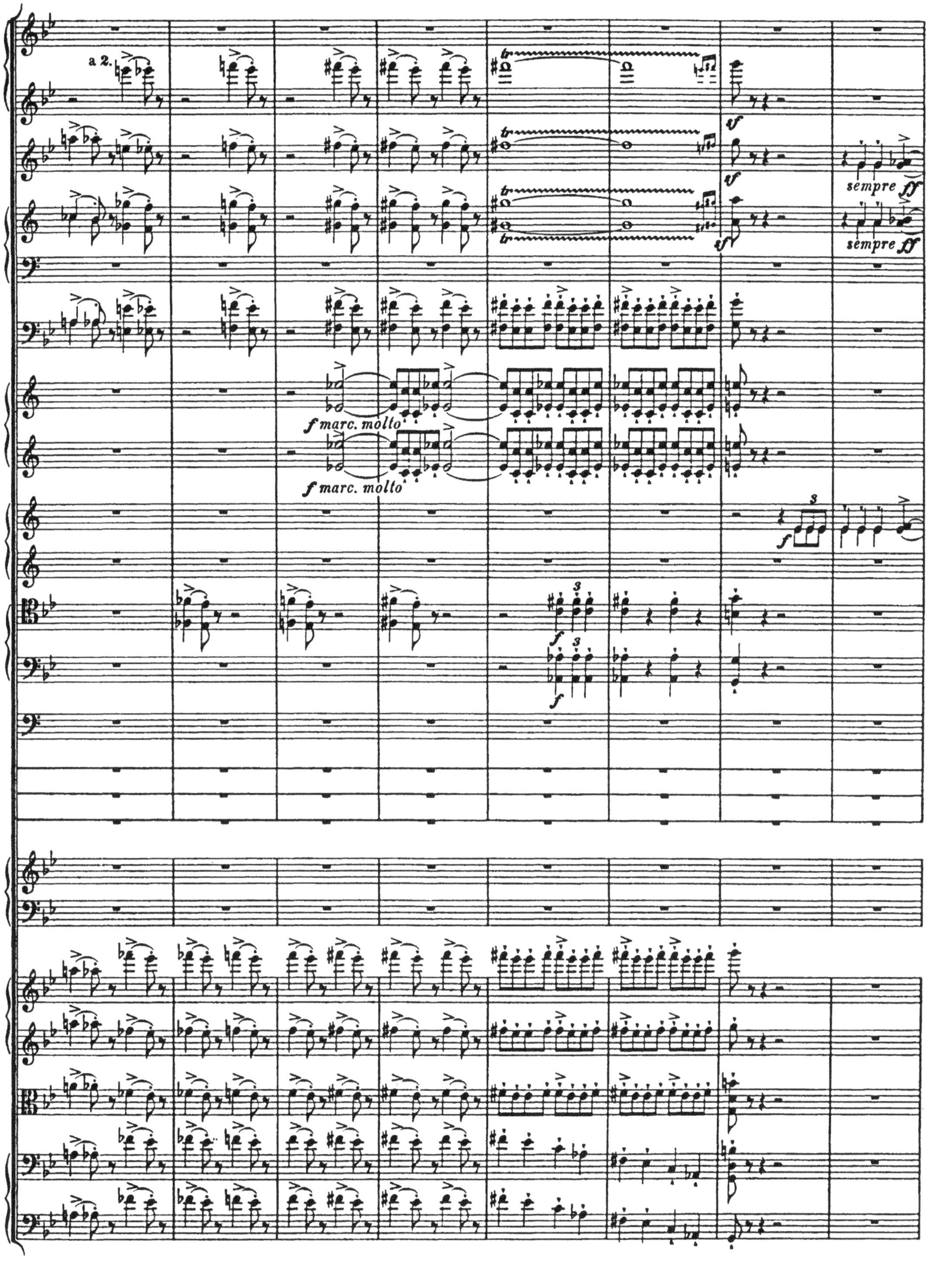
a 2.
tr
sf
sempre ff
f marc. molto
f marc. molto
f

sempre stringendo

sempre ff

sempre ff

sempre ff

sempre ff

ardito

ardito

ardito

sempre ff

sempre stringendo

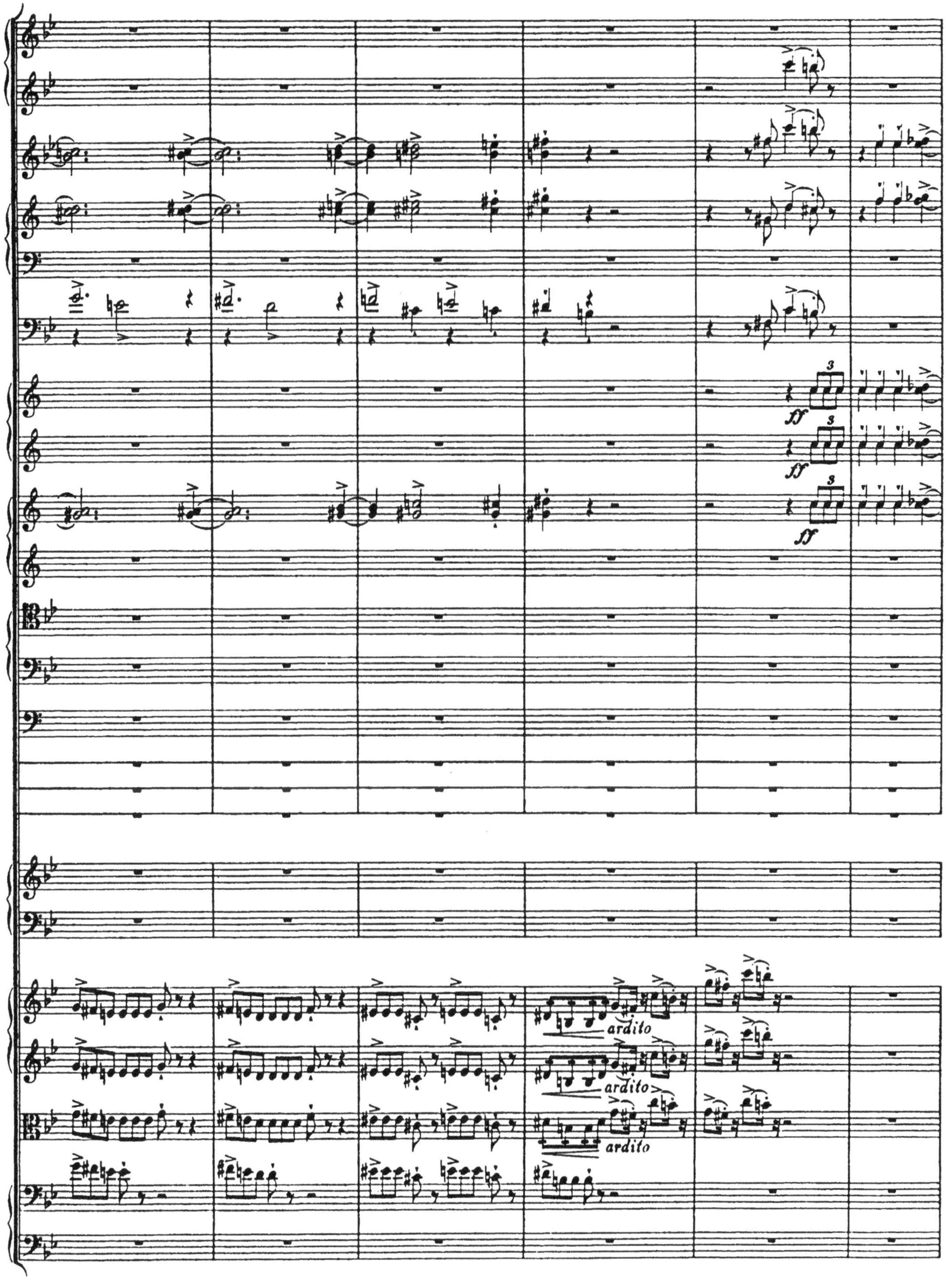
ff
ff
ff
ardito
ardito
ardito

56

sempre marcatissimo

sempre marcatissimo

sempre marcatissimo

sempre marcatissimo

a 2.

f energico

58

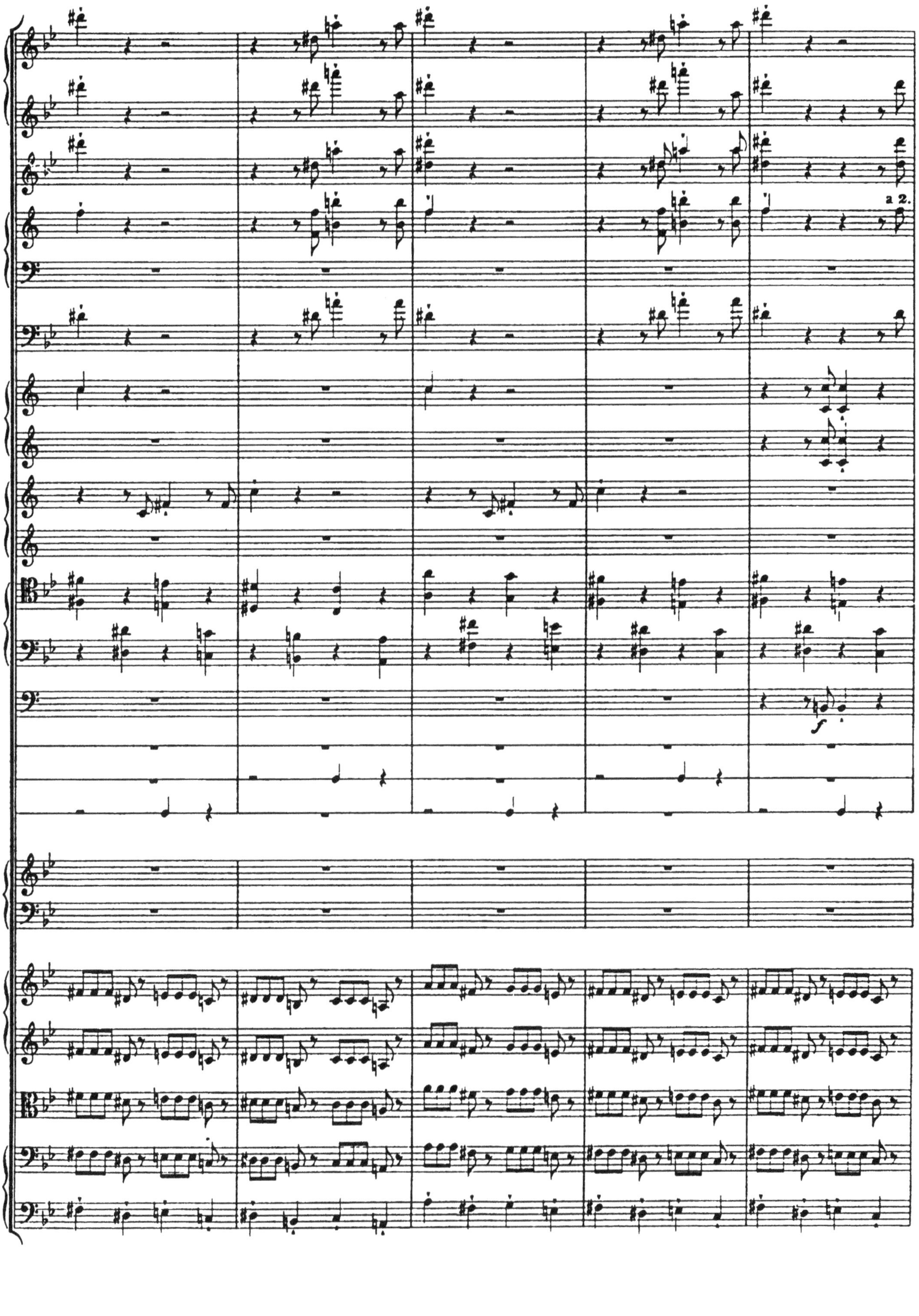
a 2.
f

Un poco meno mosso.

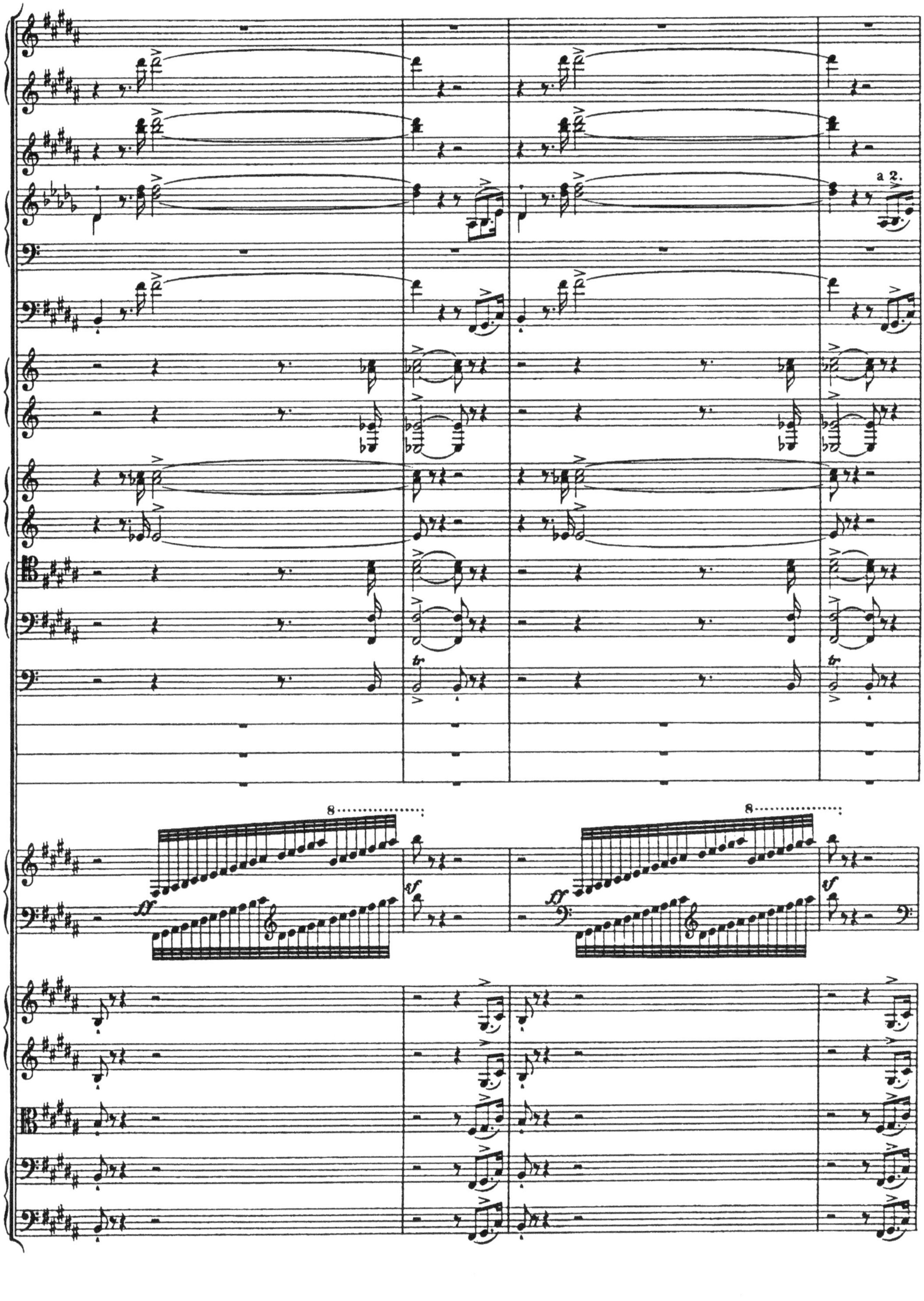
a 2.
8
ff
sf
tr

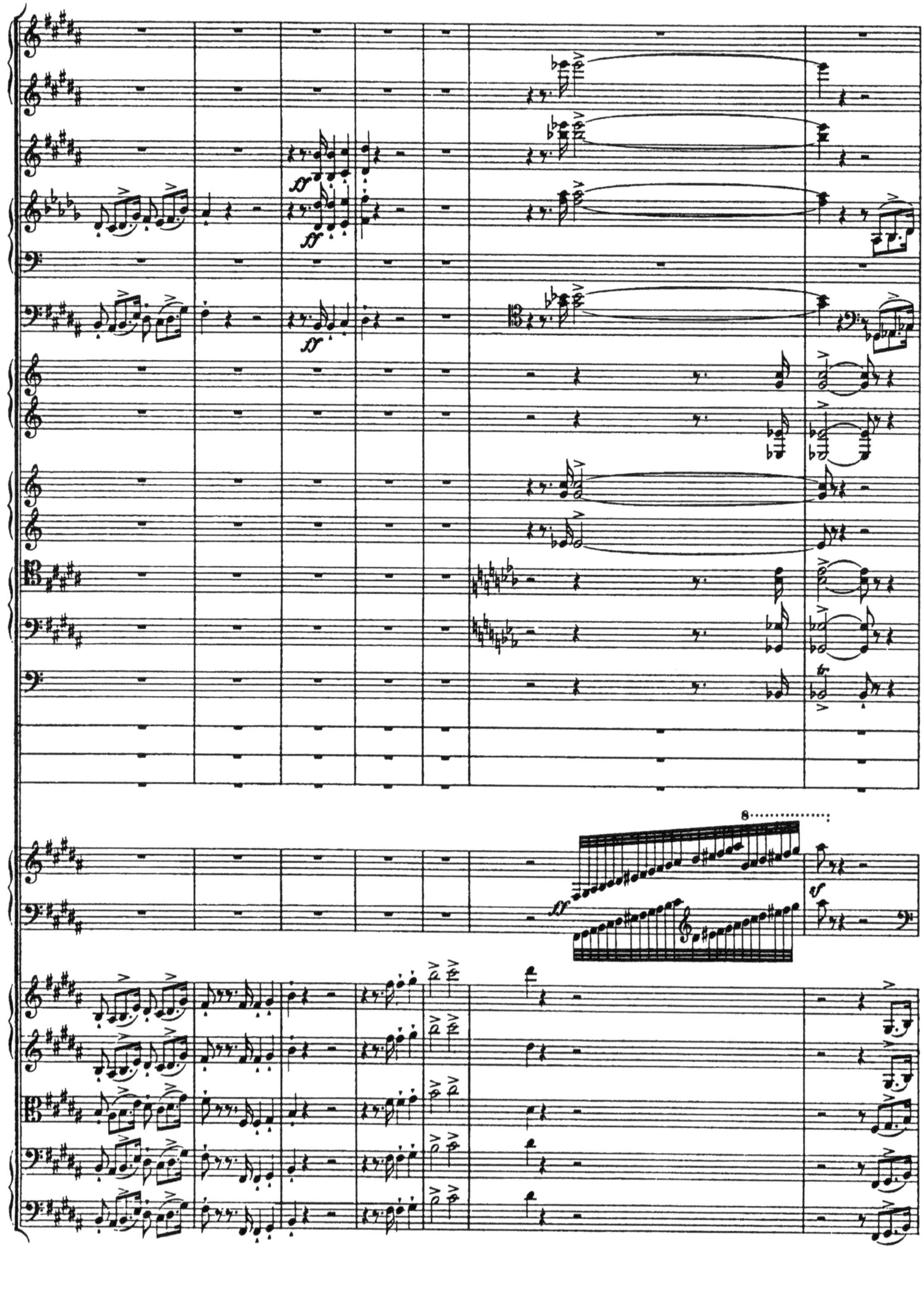

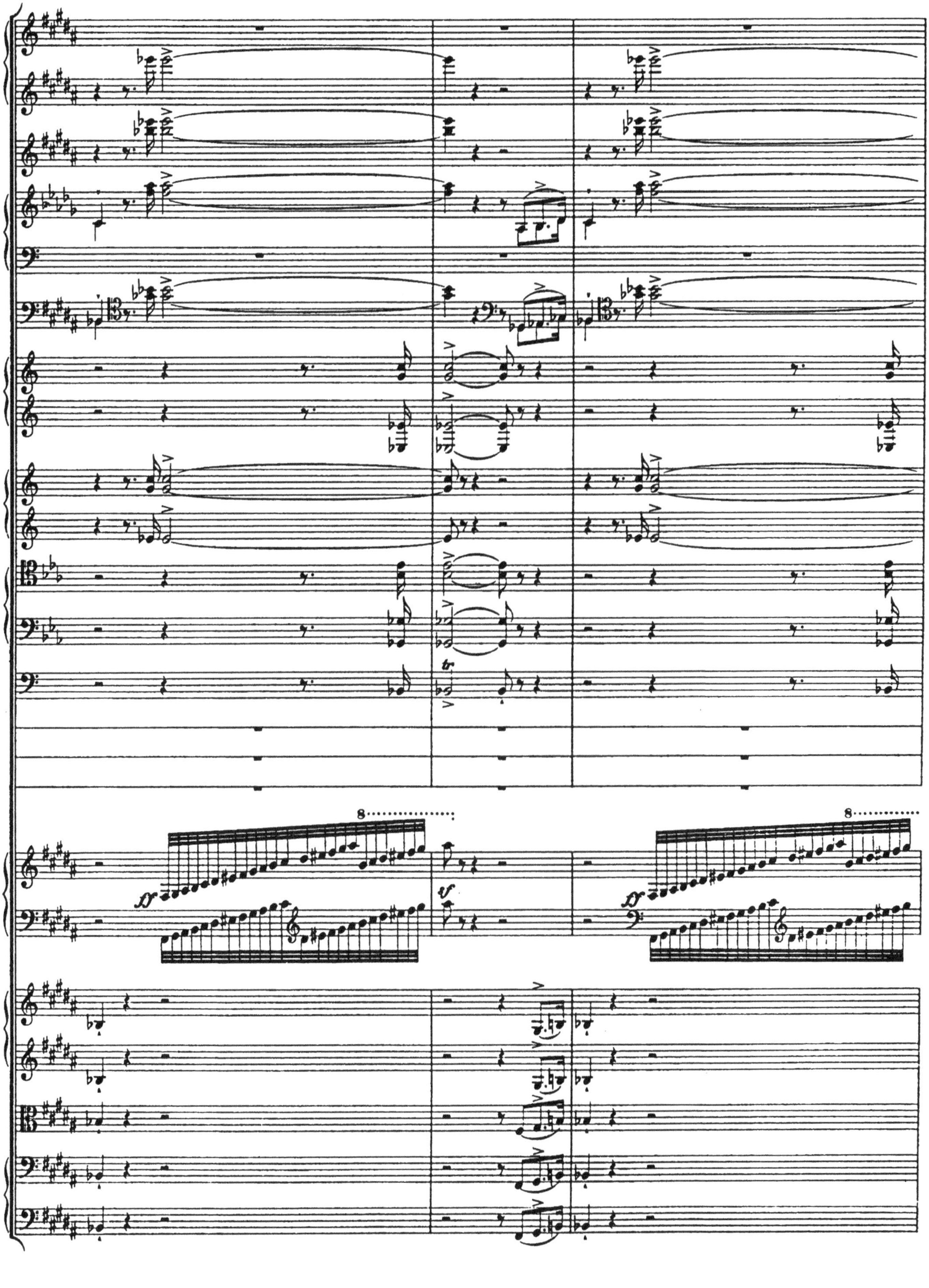

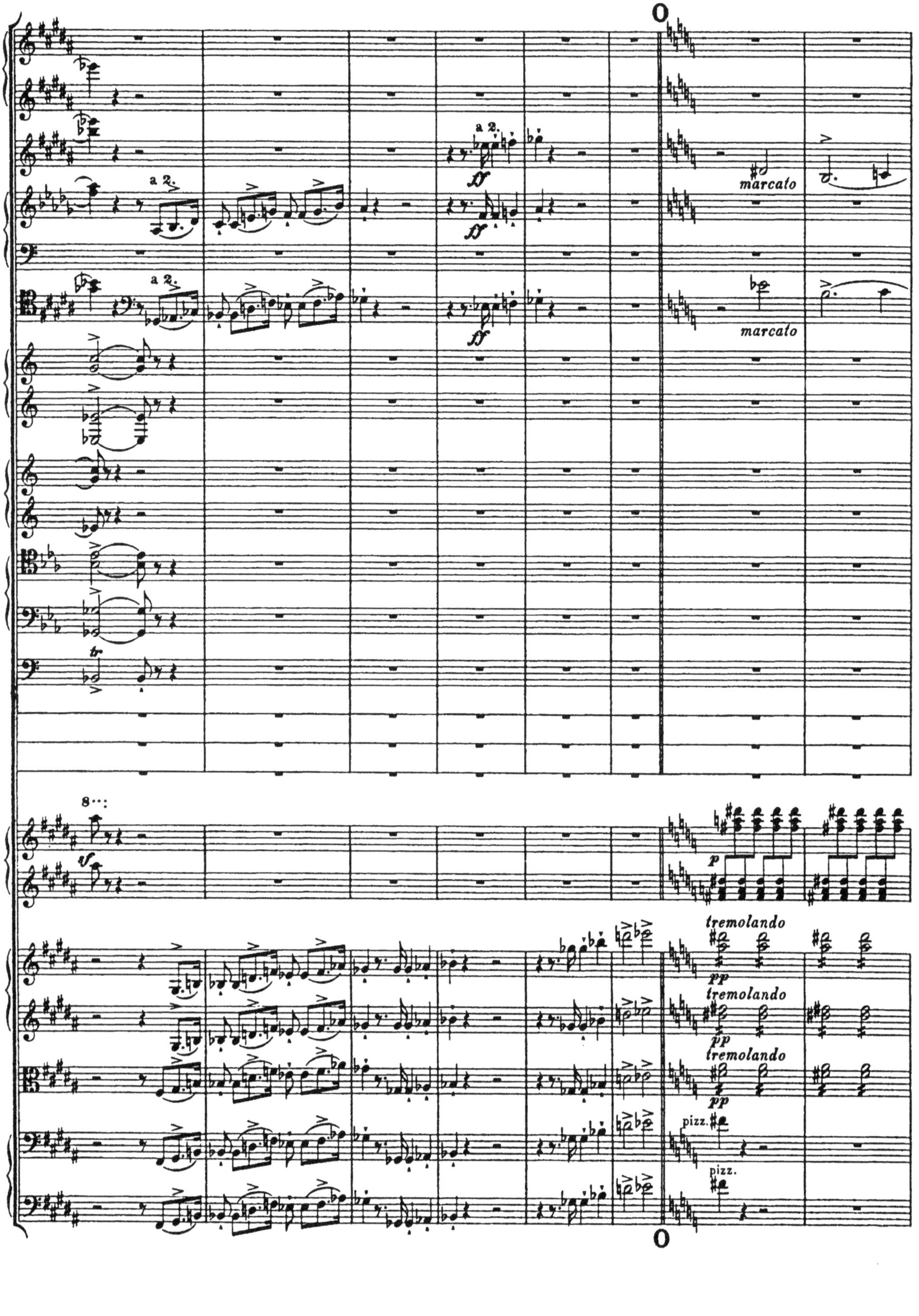
O
a 2.
ff
marcato
tr
8
sf
p
tremolando
pp
pizz.
O

cresc.
cresc.
cresc.
cresc.
cresc.
a 2.
f
a 2.
f
cresc.
cresc.
cresc.
cresc.
arco
sf
cresc.

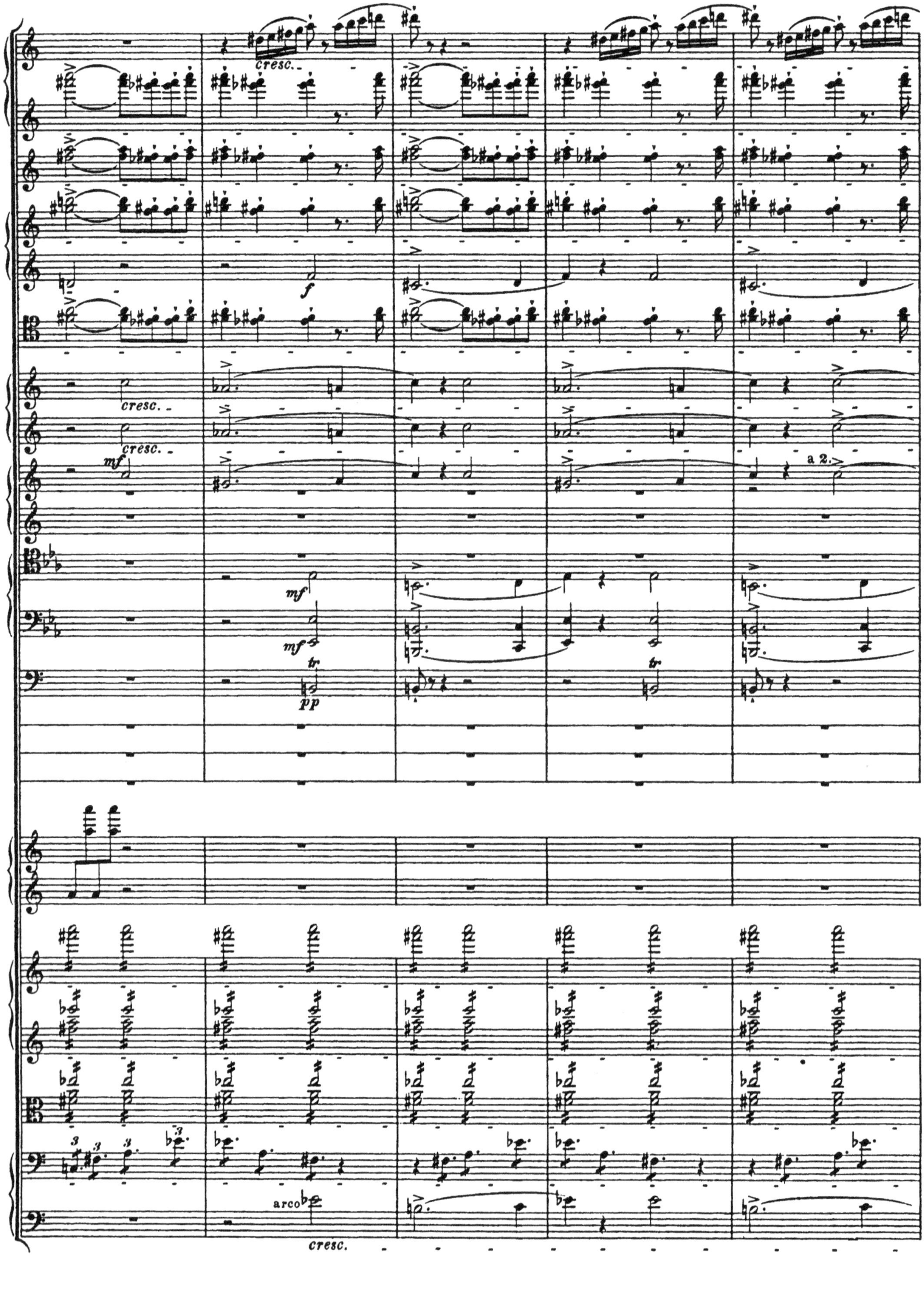
cresc.
cresc.
cresc.
mf
f
a 2.
mf
mf
tr
pp
tr
arco
cresc.

a 2.
ff
a 2.
ff
ff
ff
a 2.
ff
ff
ff
ff
a 2.
ff
ff
tr
cresc.
f
ardito
sf
ff
ardito
sf
ff
ardito
sf
ff
ardito
ff

68

a 2.
a 2.
Muta B in H, H in D.
mf
sempre ff
sempre ff
sempre ff
sempre ff
sempre ff

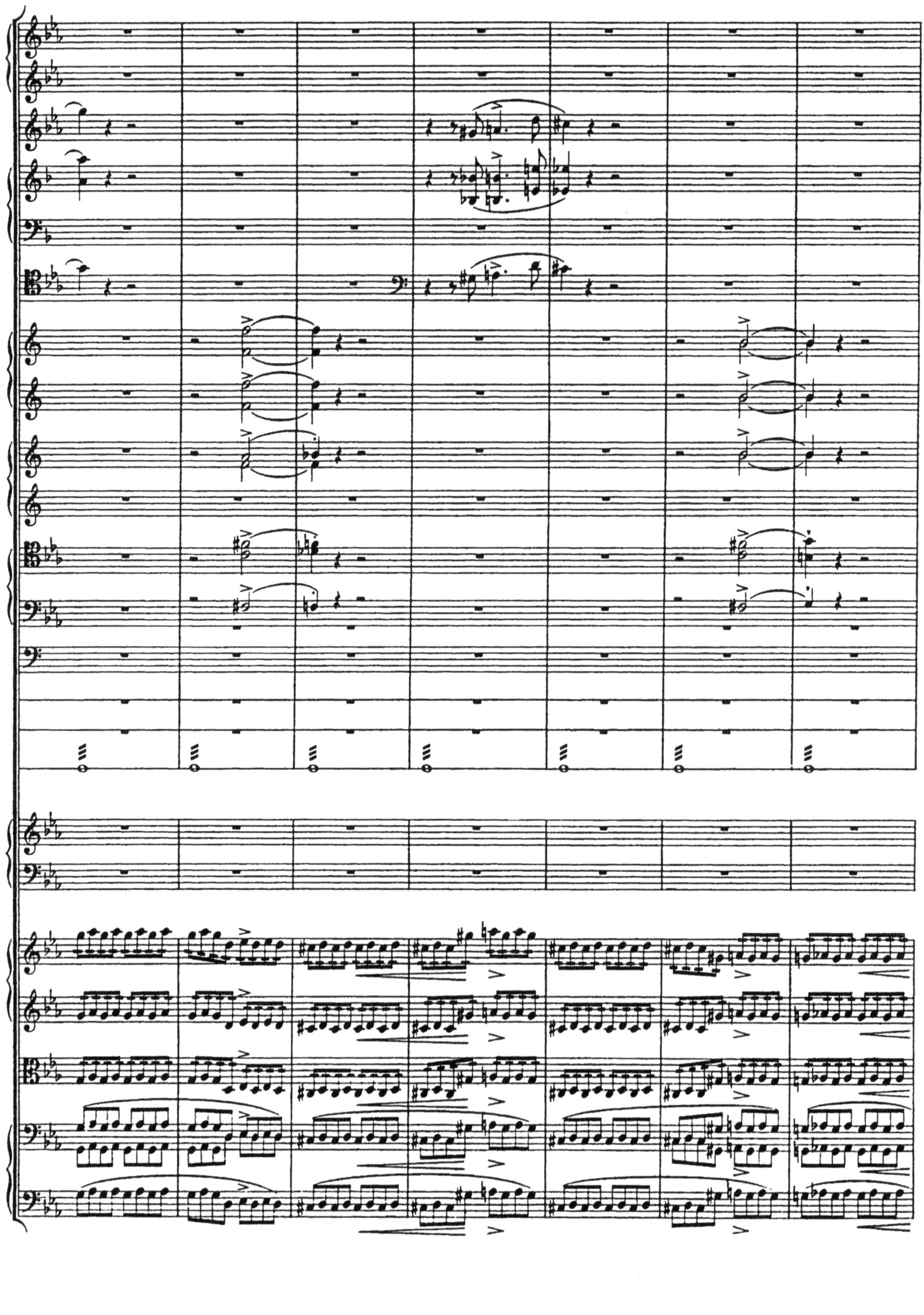

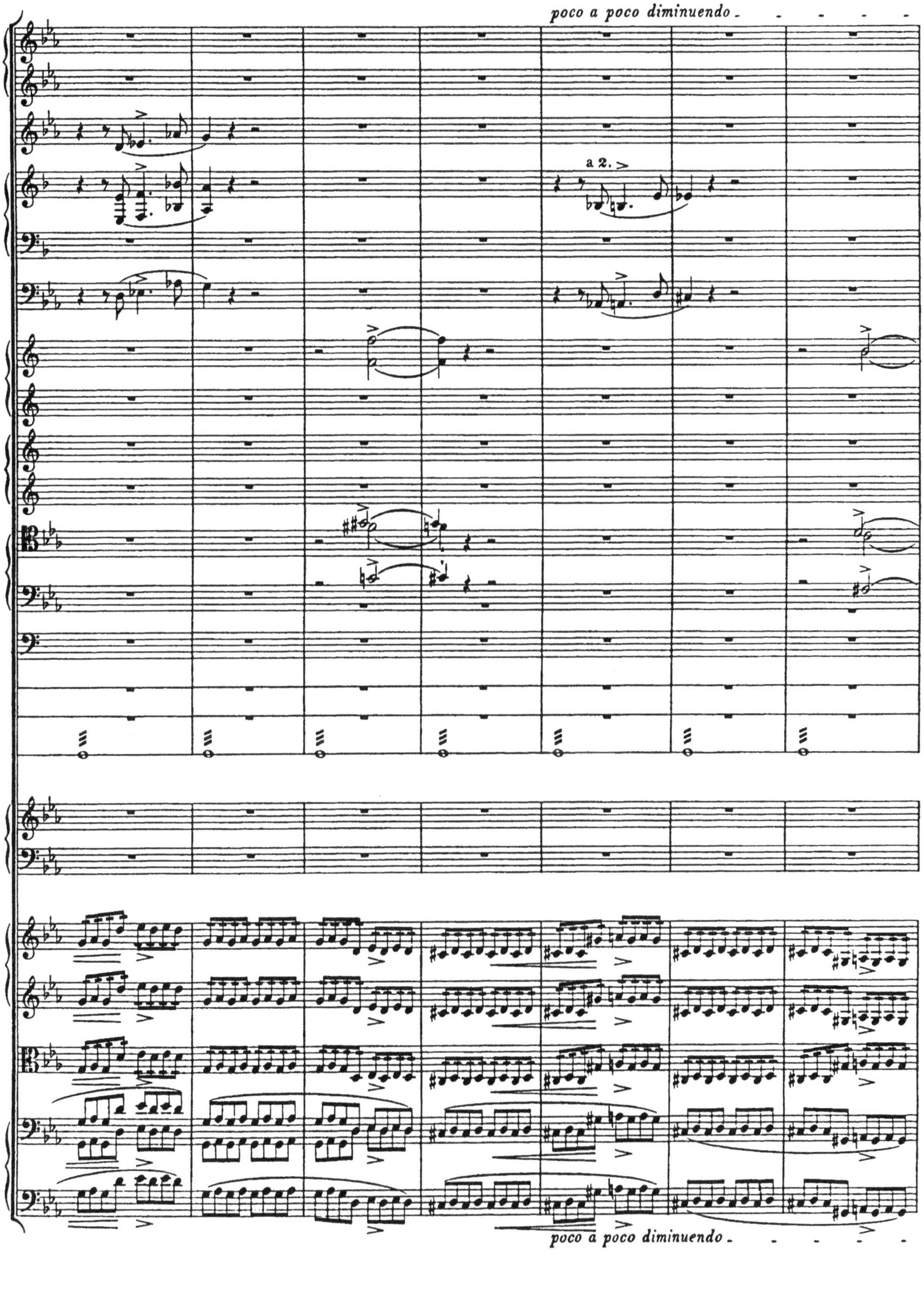
poco a poco diminuendo
a 2.
poco a poco diminuendo

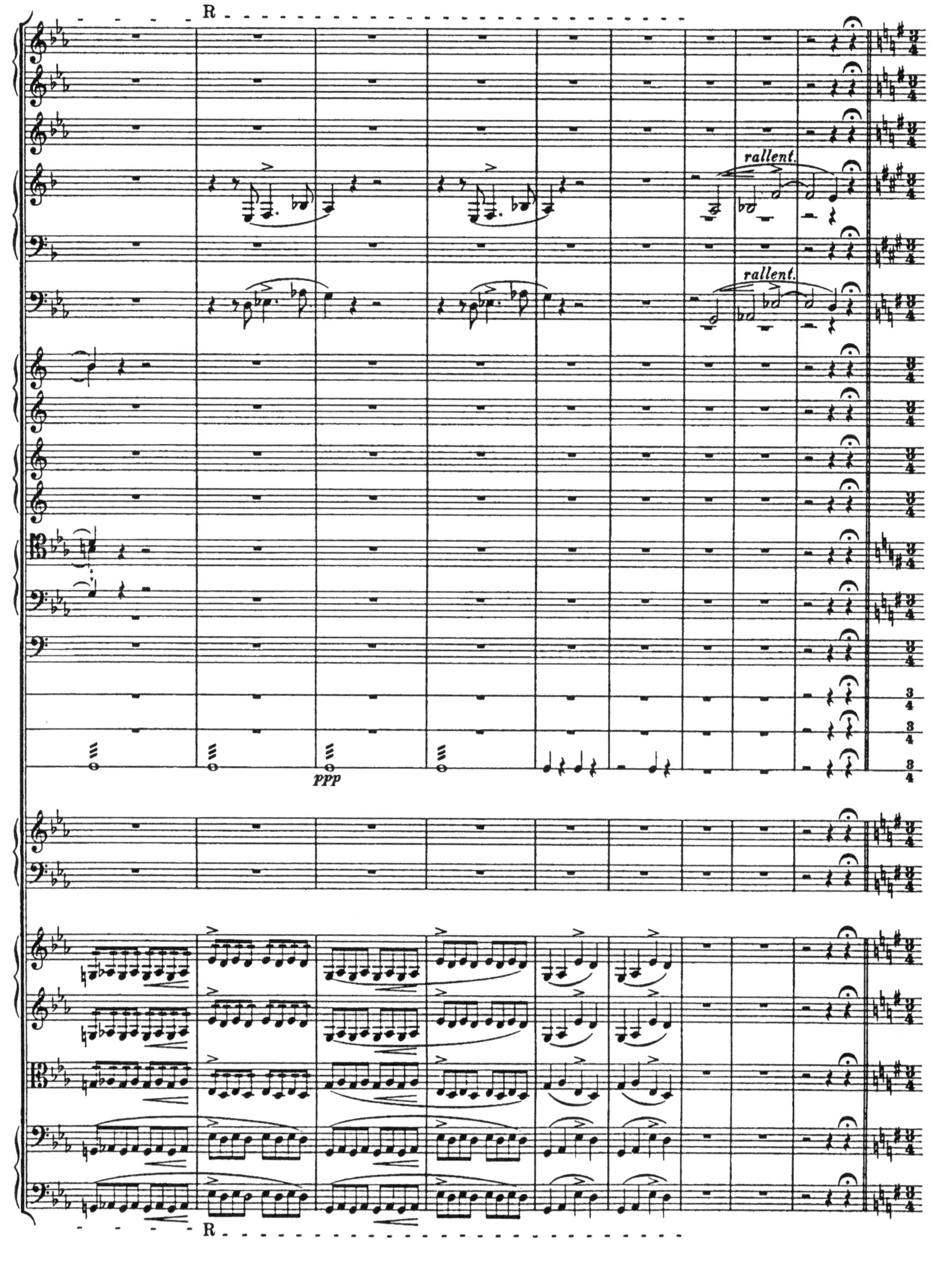
R
rallent.
rallent.
ppp
R

Andante religioso.
espressivo
mf
mf
mf
1. Posaune cantabile.
mp espressivo
dim.
mp
dim.
Andante religioso.

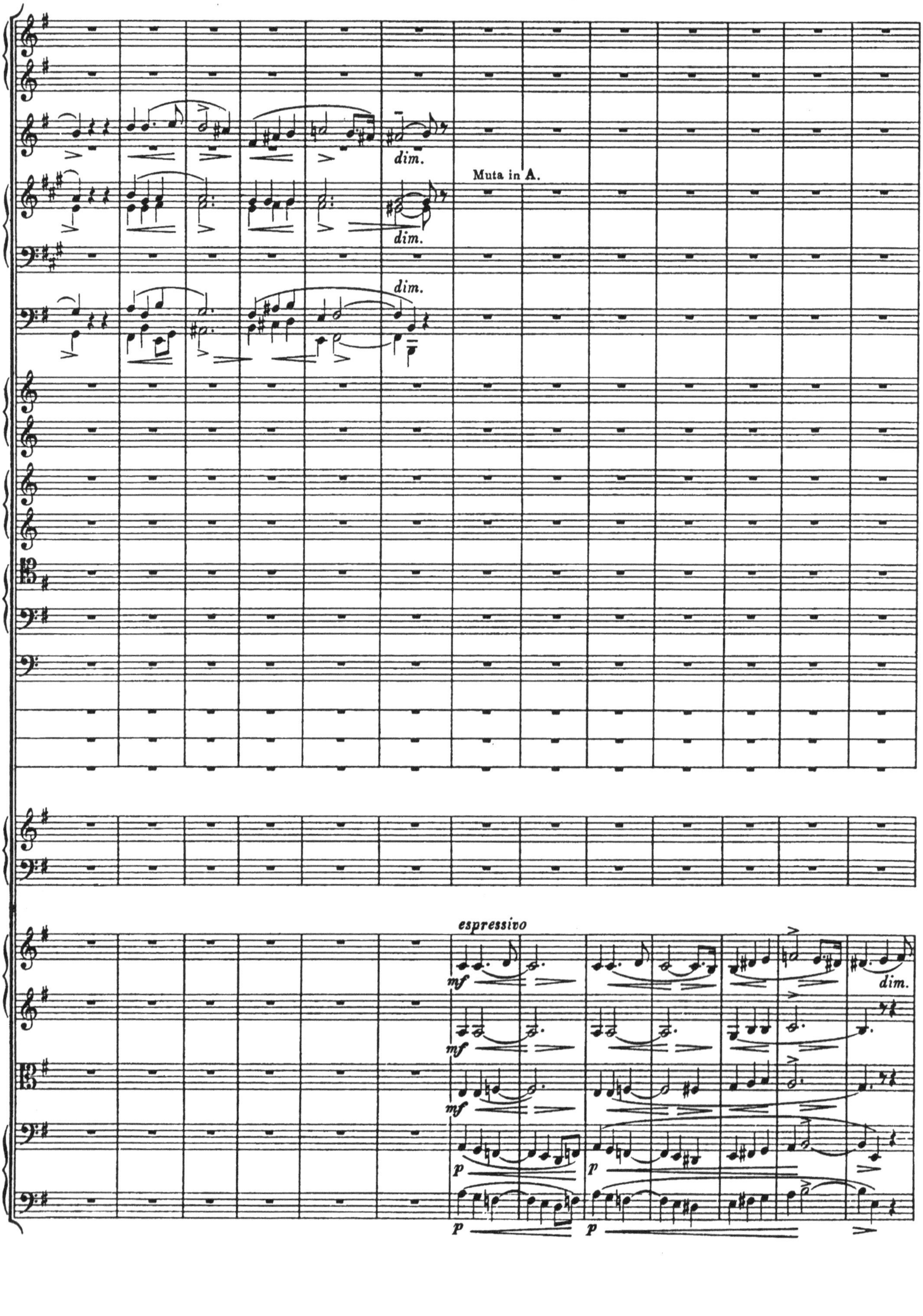
dim.
dim.
Muta in A.
dim.
espressivo
mf
dim.
mf
mf
p
p

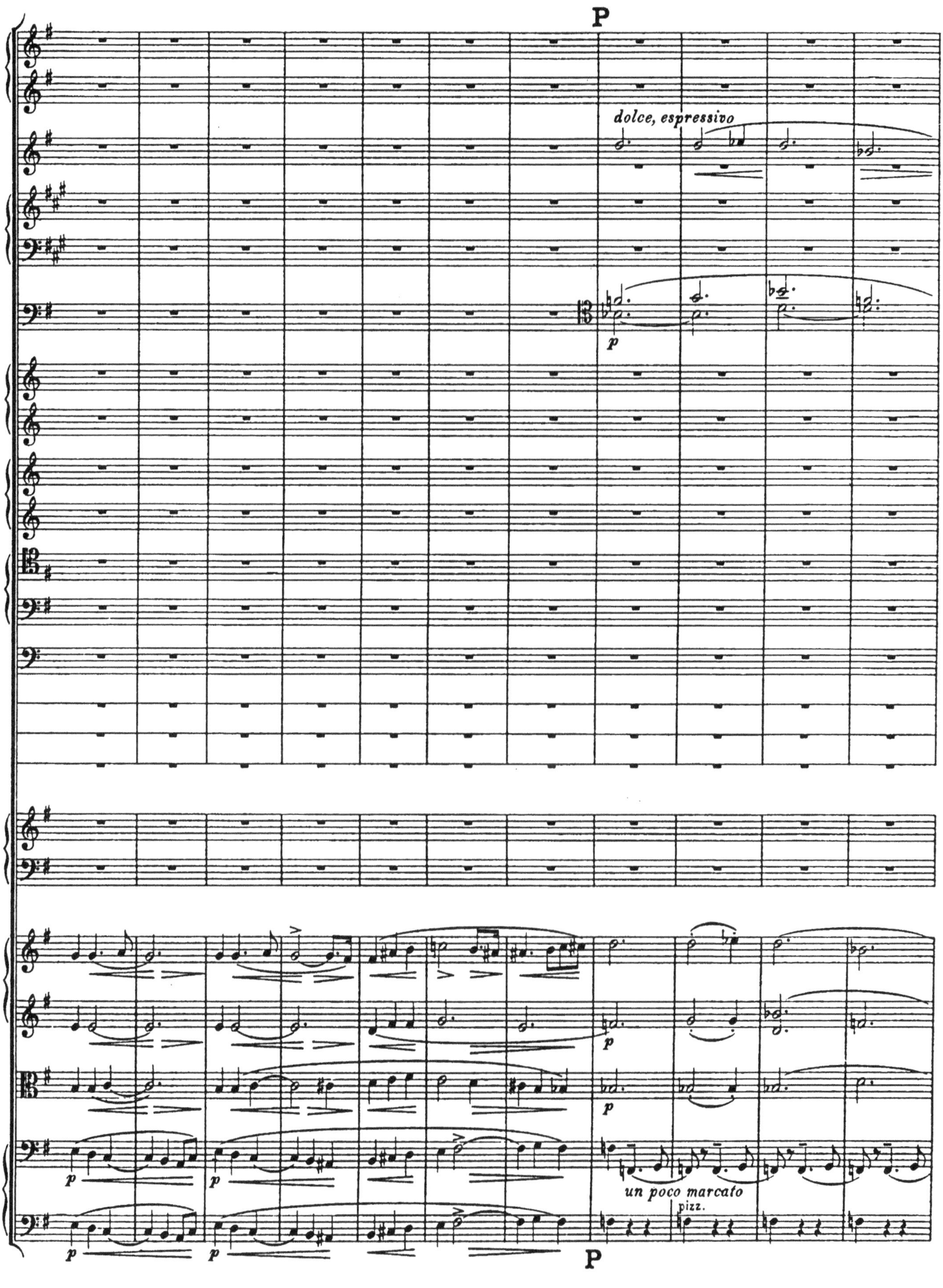
P
dolce, espressivo
p
p
p
p
p
un poco marcato
pizz.
P

poco riten.
Allegro moderato. (Alla breve.)
pp
pp
mf molto tranquillo
con Sordino
pp tranquillo
con Sordino
pp
pp tranquillo
arco
pp tranquillo
poco riten.
Allegro moderato. (Alla breve.)

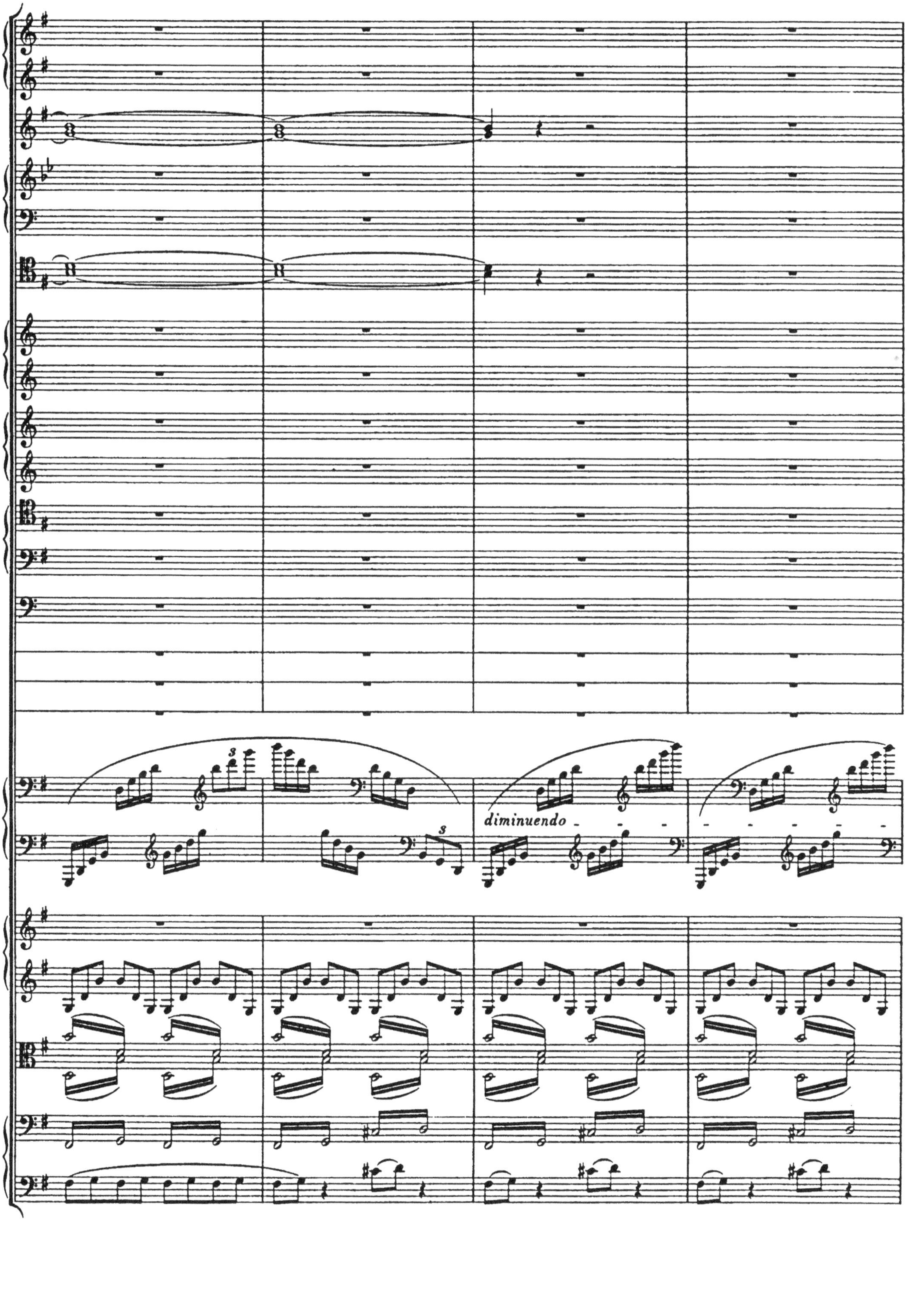
diminuendo

dolce, tranquillo molto

dolciss., tranquillo molto

6 erste Violinen allein.
6 first violins soli.
6 premiers violons seuls.

pp
con Sordino

pp
con Sordino

pp
con Sordino

pp

pizz.

* Die 3 ersten Violinen Flageolet. *The 3 first violins in harmonics.* Les 3 premiers violons en sons harmoniques.

un poco ritenuto il tempo

un poco ritenuto il tempo

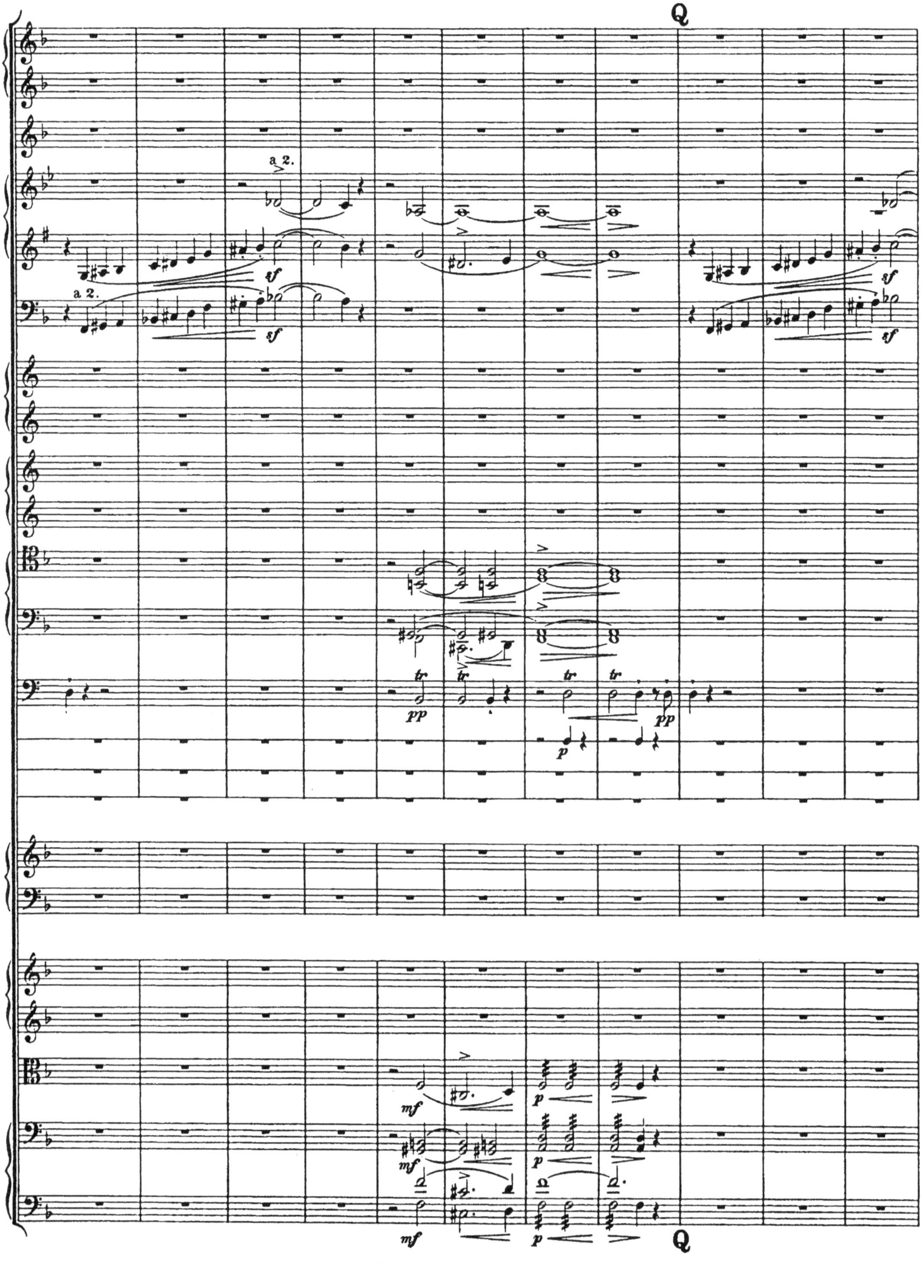
Q
a 2.
a 2.
sf
sf
sf
sf
tr
pp
pp
p
mf
mf
mf
p
p
p
Q

Allegro moderato.

Allegro moderato.

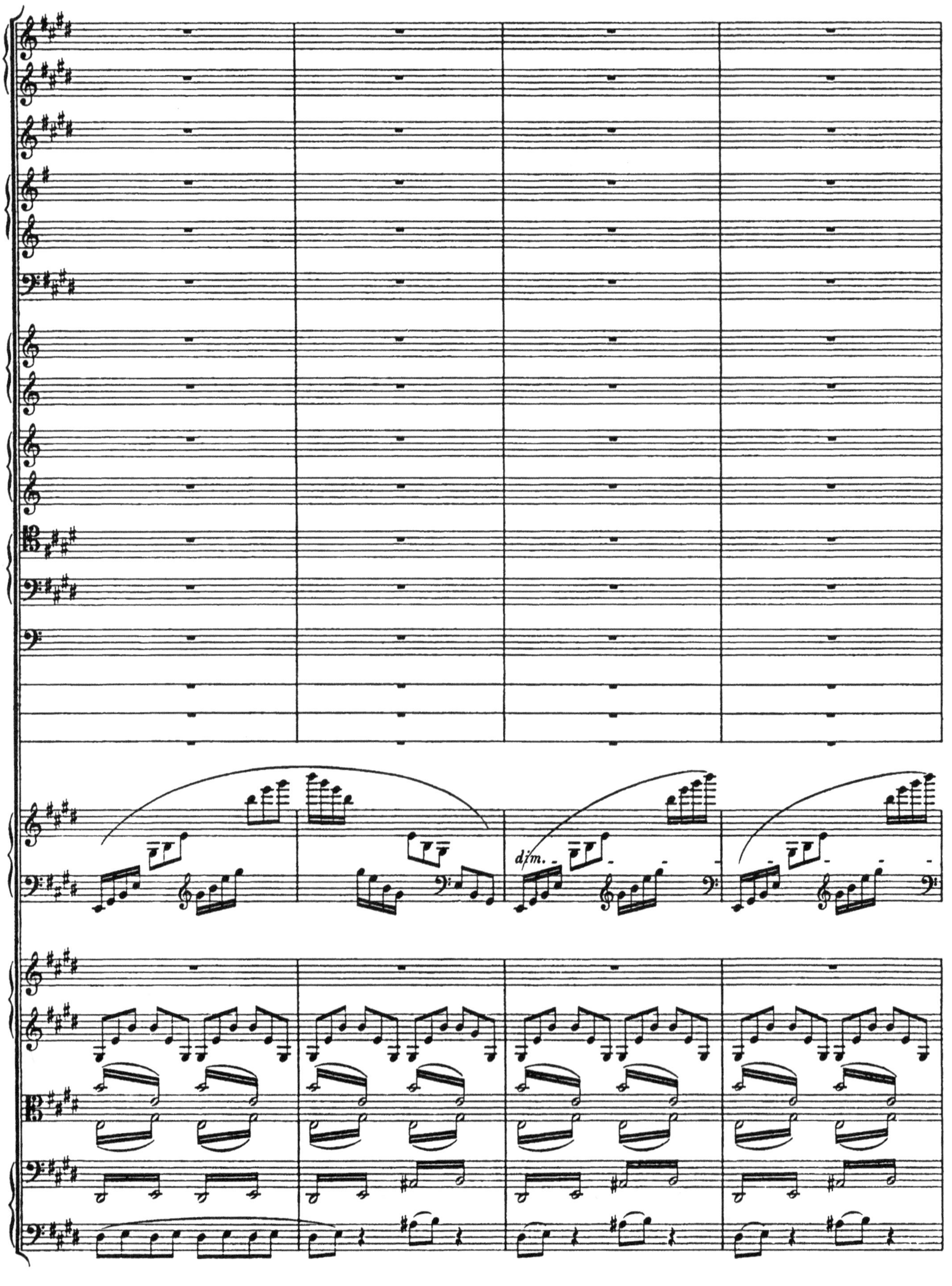
dim.

* Die 3 ersten Violinen Flageolet.   *The 3 first violins in harmonics.*   Les 3 premiers violons en sons harmoniques.

84

un poco ritenuto il tempo

Muta H in B, D in Es.

R

ritenuto molto
Allegro. Poco a poco più di moto.
a 2.
p
Muta in B.
in B.
marcato
mf
perdendo
marcato
mf
p dolce
p dolce
senza sord.
dolce, con grazia
senza sord.
p
senza sord.
p
pizz.
p
pizz.
p
ritenuto molto
Allegro. Poco a poco più di moto.

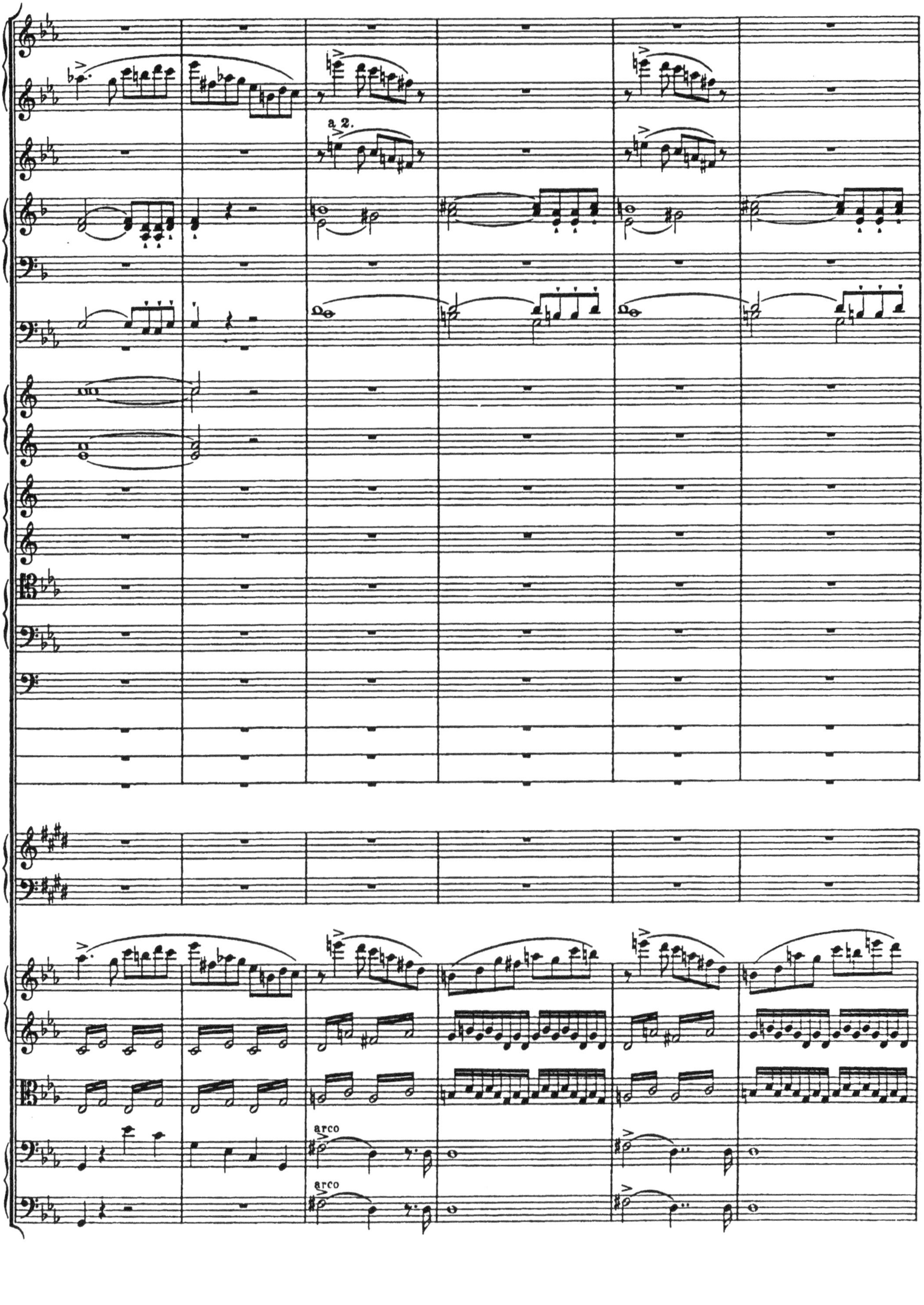
a 2.
arco
arco

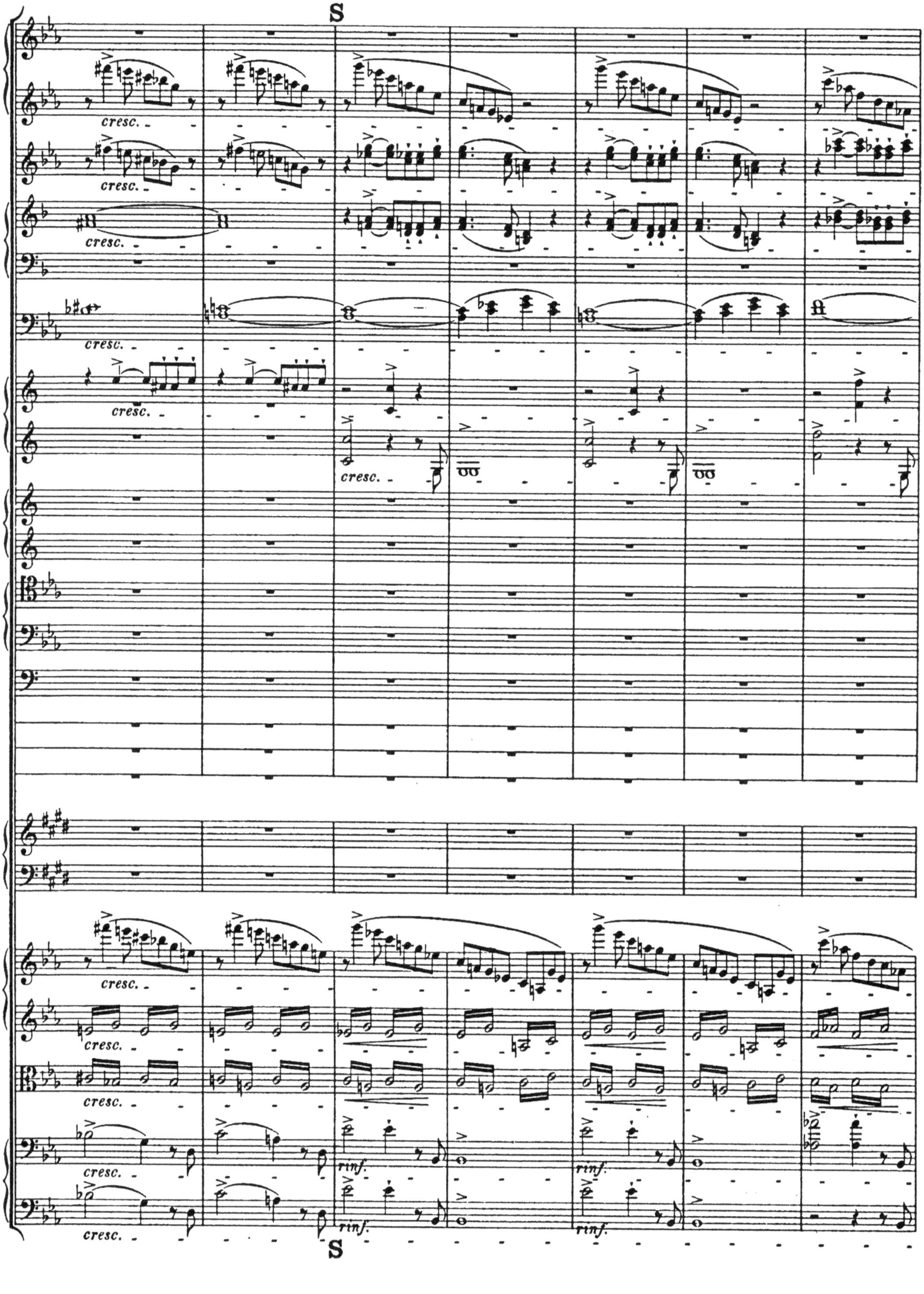
S
cresc.
rinf.
S

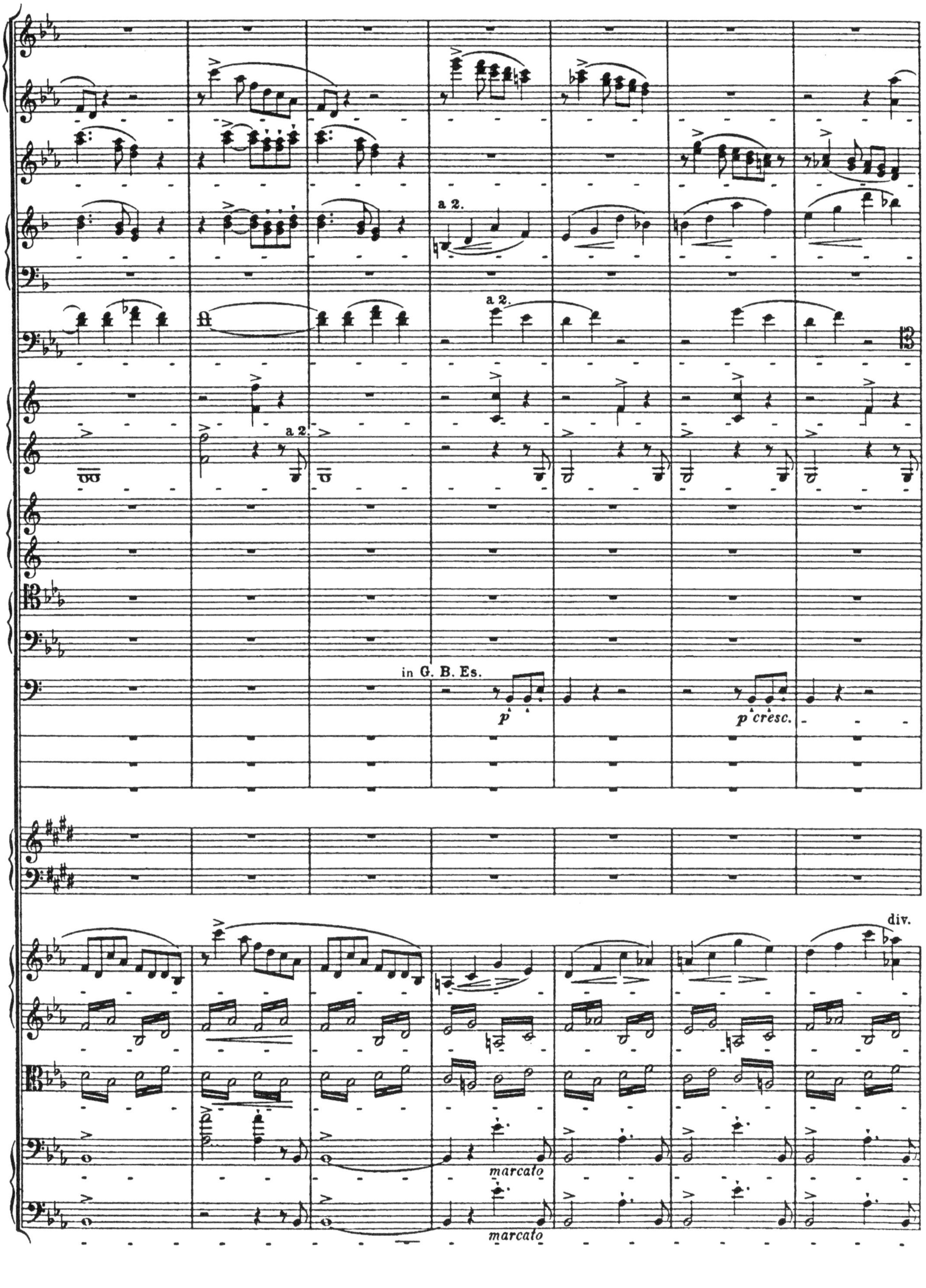
a 2.
a 2.
a 2.
in G. B. Es.
p
p cresc.
div.
marcato
marcato

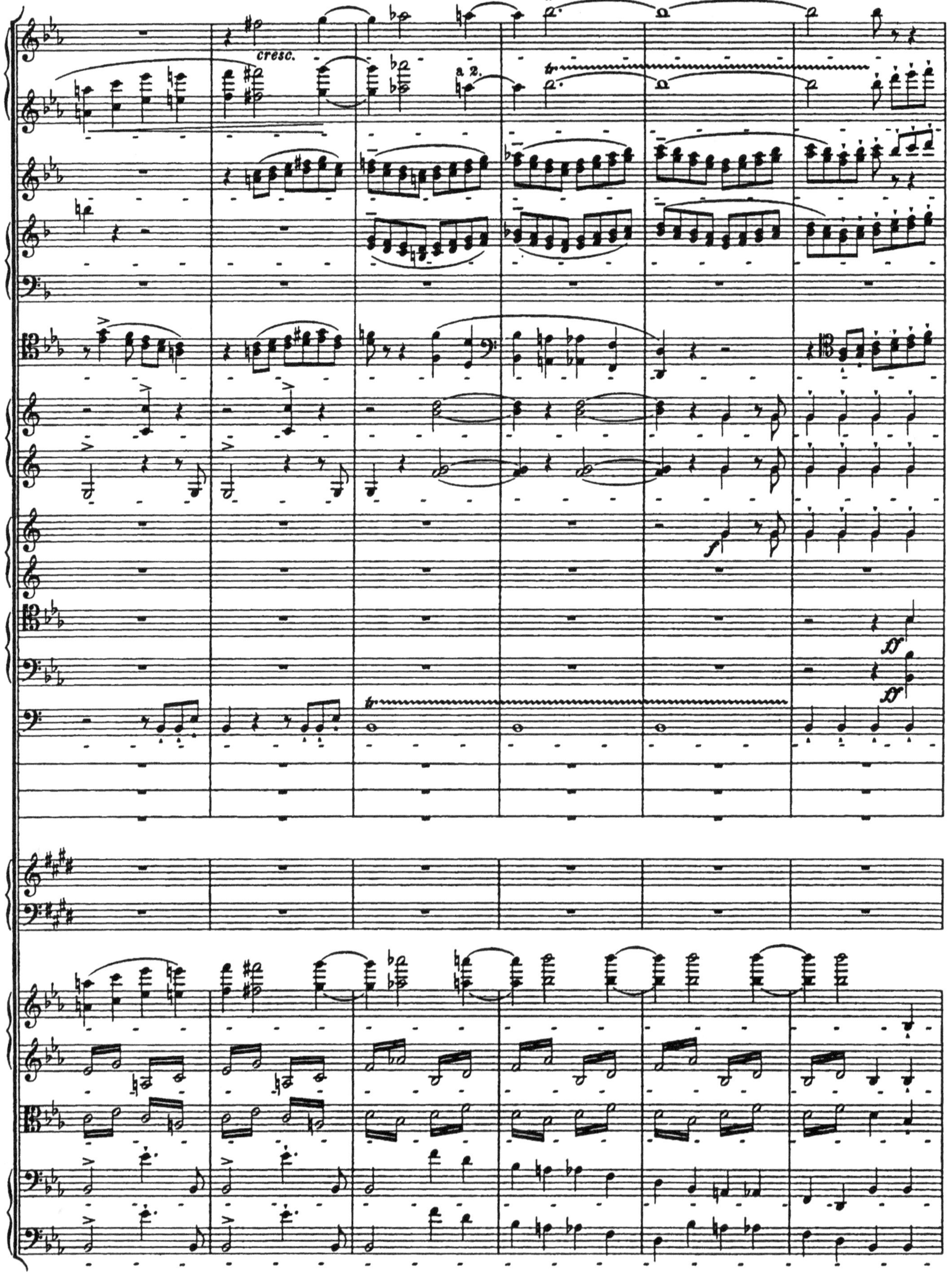
tr
cresc.
a 2.
f
ff

Allegro animato e brioso.

Allegro animato e brioso.
NB. Die Hörner-, Trompeten- und Posaunen-Fanfaren mässig, aber nicht roh.
The horn-, trumpet- and trombone-fanfares somewhat prominent, but without coarseness.
Le son des cors, trompettes et trombones modéré, mais pas rude.

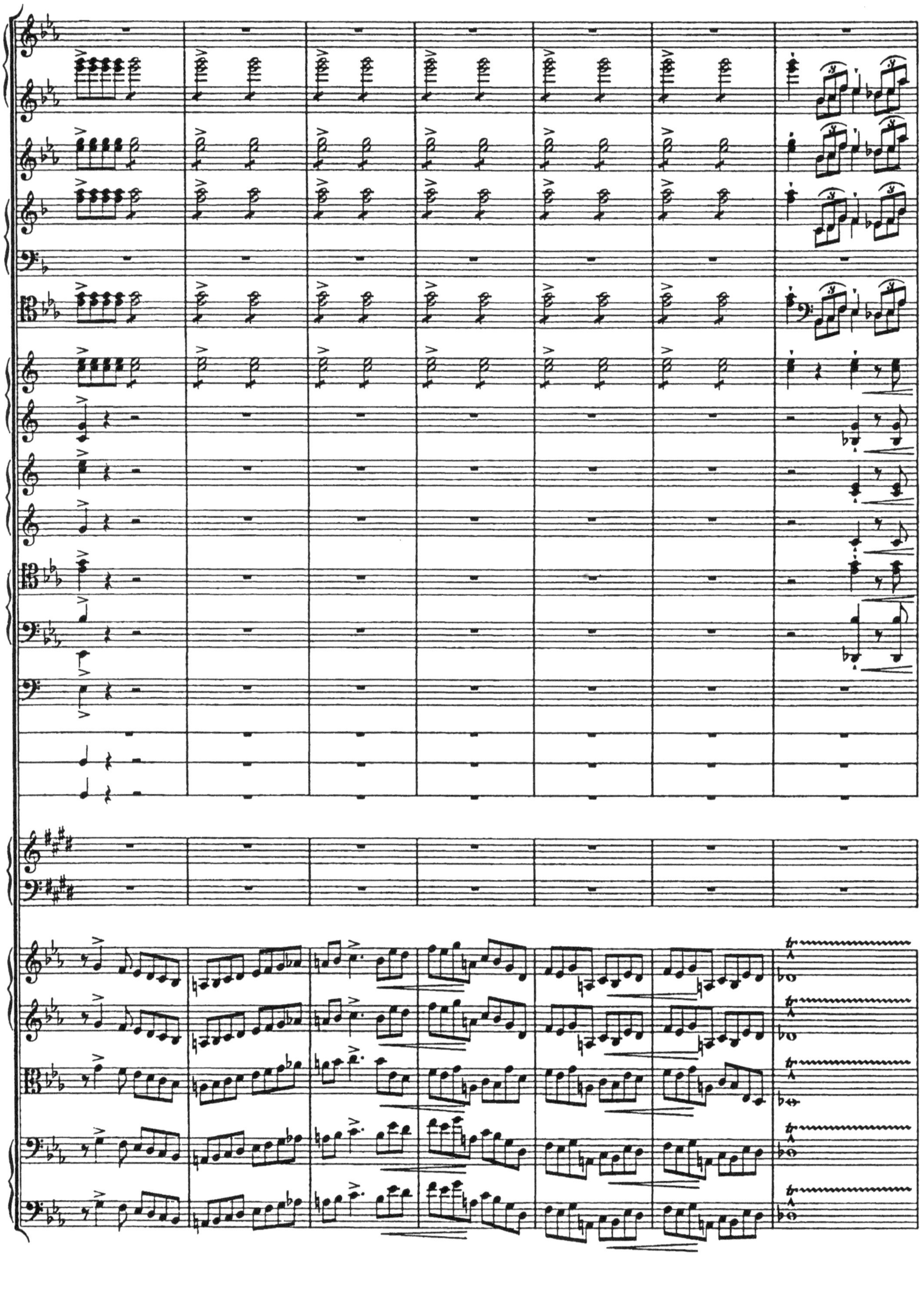

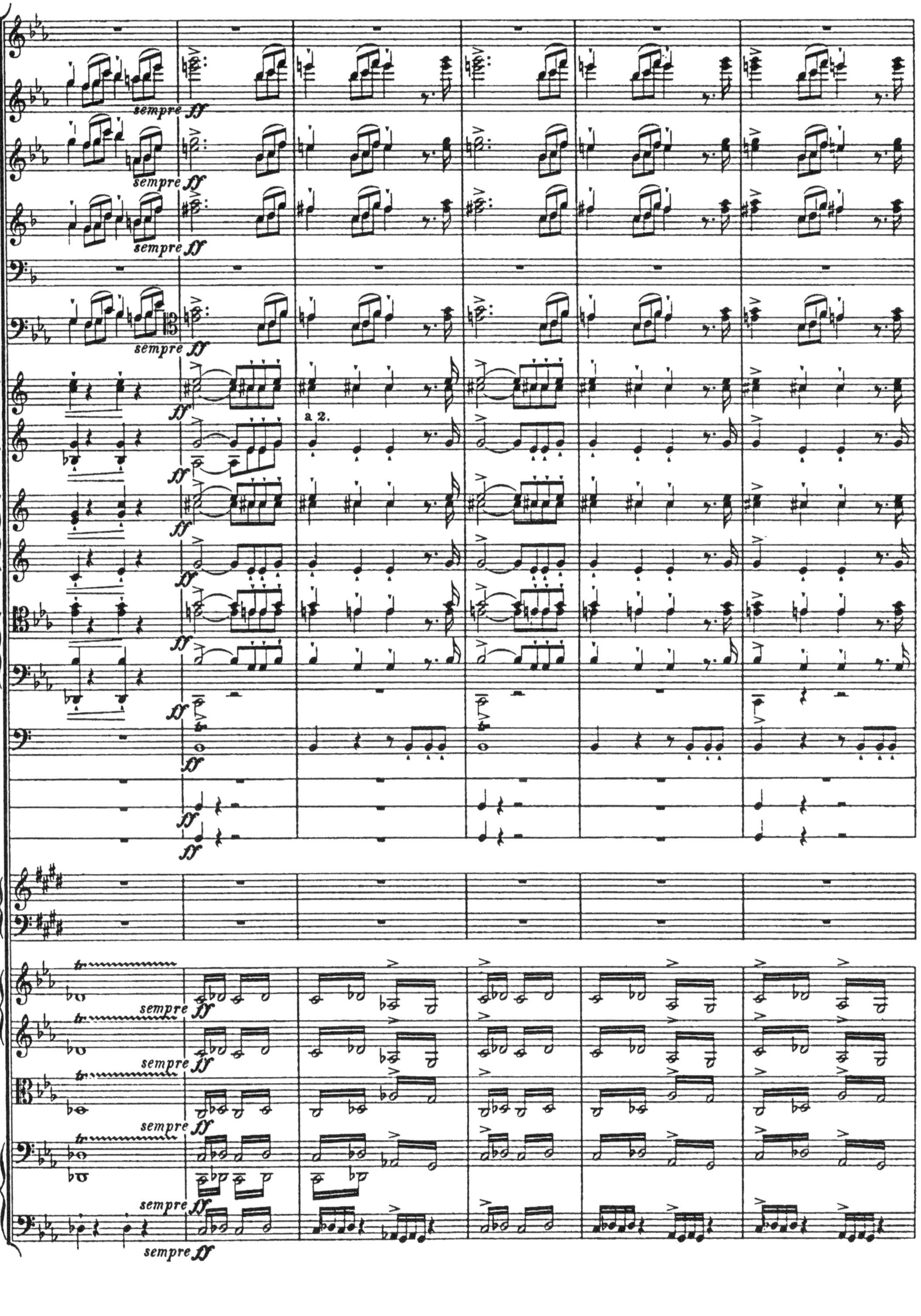
sempre ff
a 2.

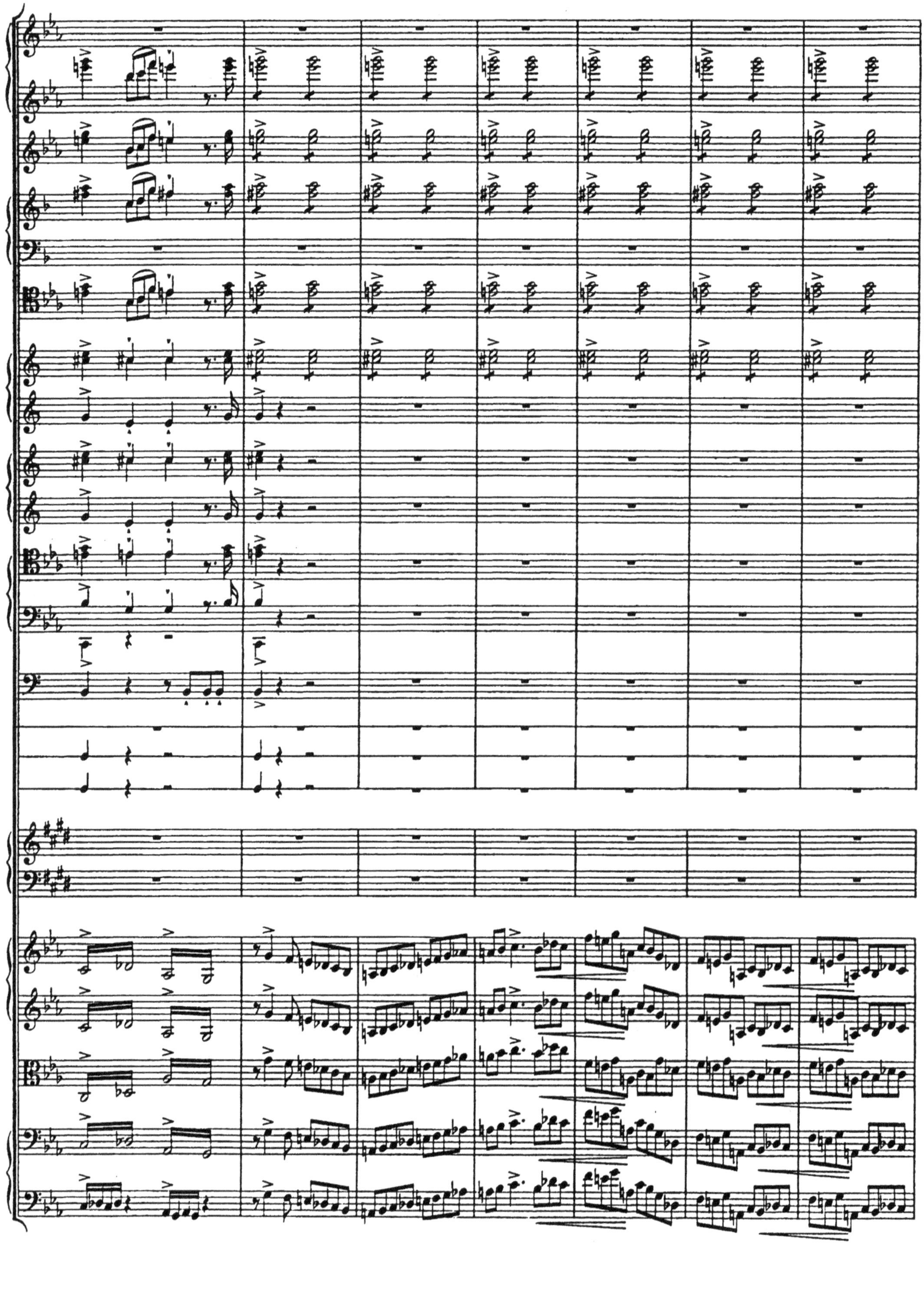

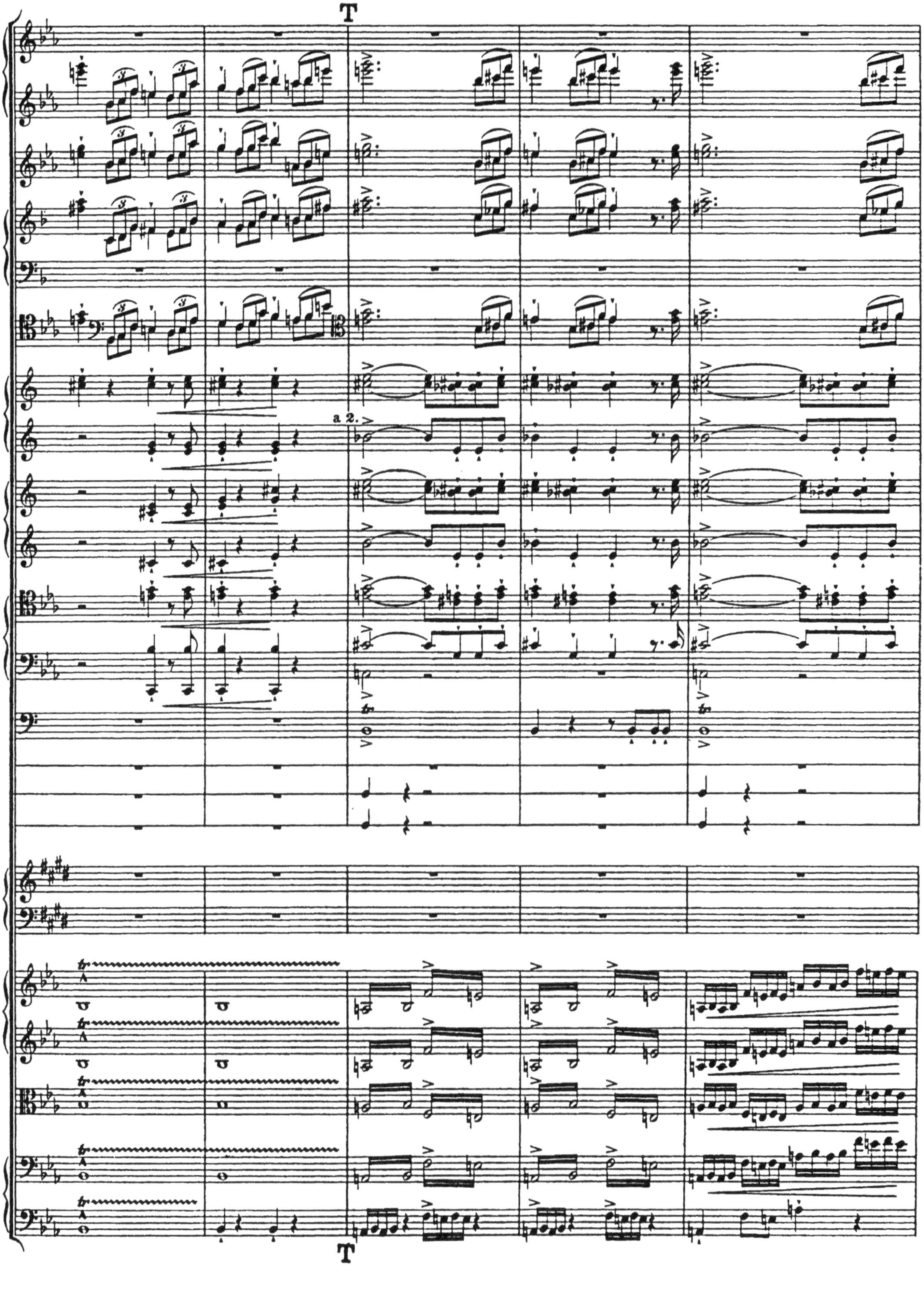
T
a 2.
tr
T

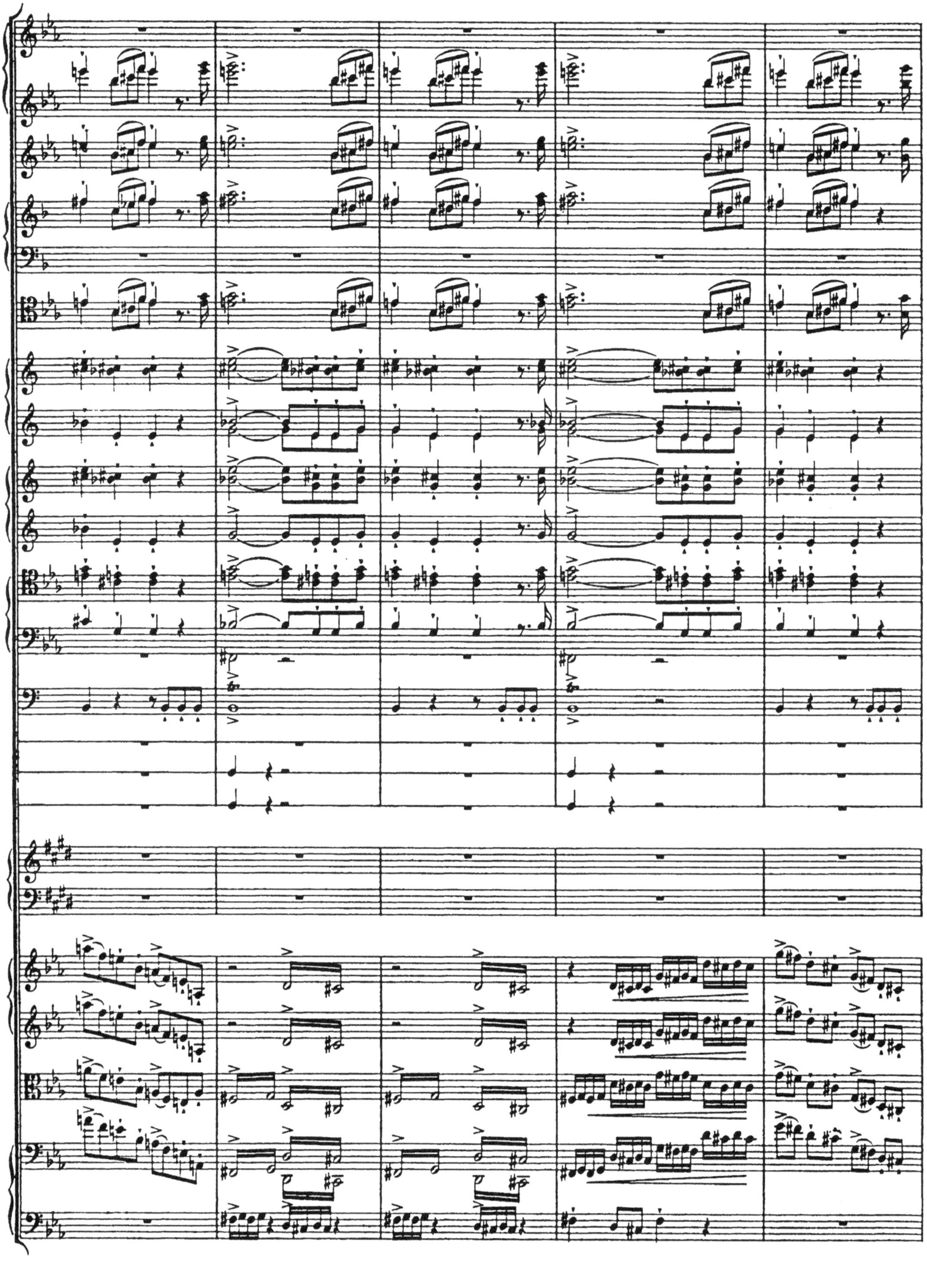

Muta in A.
a 2.
ff sempre
ff sempre
ff sempre
ff sempre
a 2.
tr
tr
ff sempre
ff sempre
ff sempre
ff sempre
ff sempre

(senza rallentare)

dolce, con grazia

in A.

Muta in F.

Muta in F.

Muta in C.

(senza rallentare)

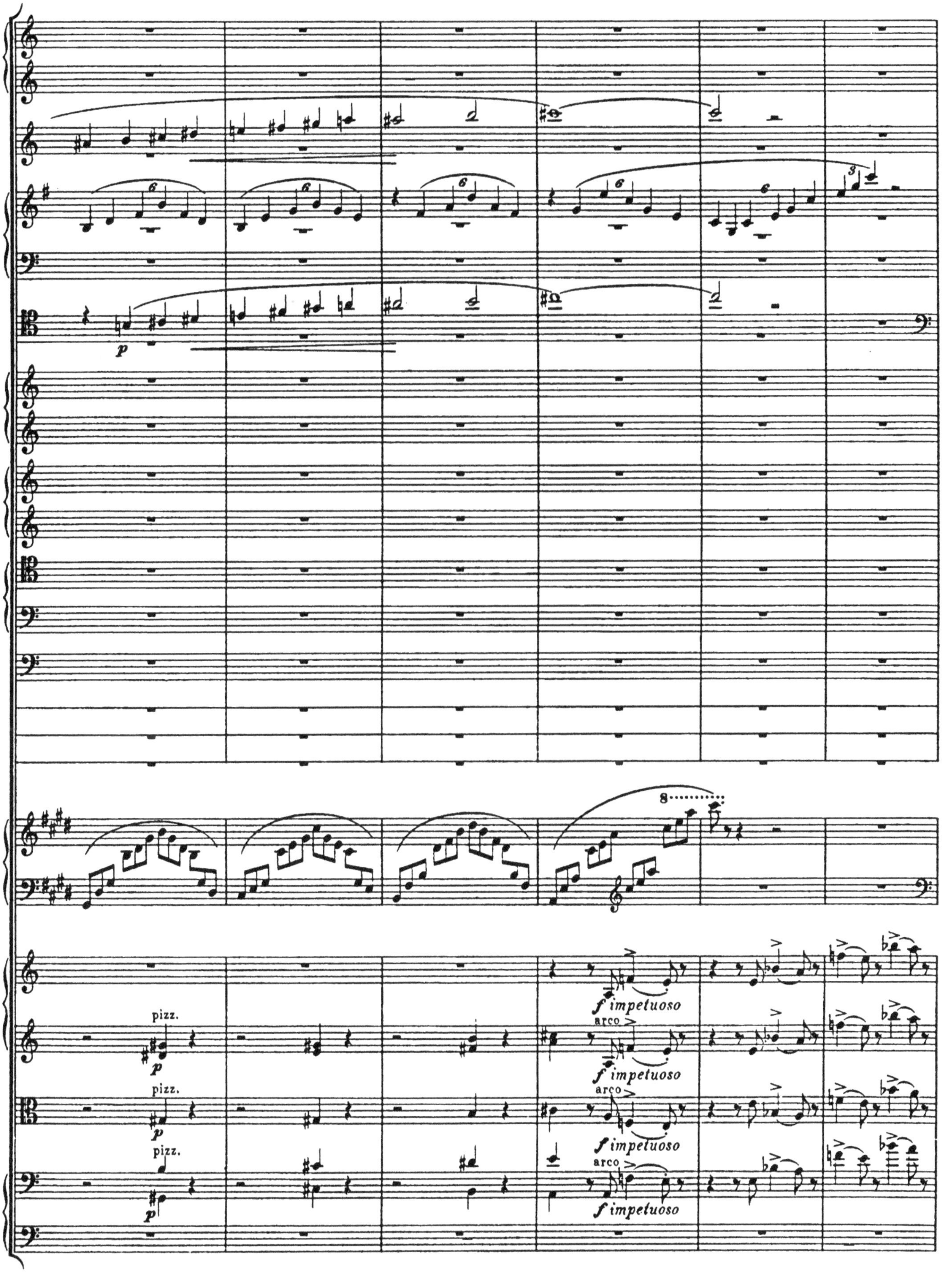

p
8
pizz.
p
arco
f impetuoso

p
a 2.
p
a 2.
p
a 2.
p
pizz.
p
arco
f impetuoso
arco
f impetuoso
arco
f impetuoso

U
a 2.
p
in F. a 2.
marcato
p un poco marcato
p un poco marcato
ff
ff
p
p
arco
p
U

agitato cresc. molto
a 2.
agitato cresc. molto
agitato cresc. molto
cresc.
cresc.
cresc.
in F. a 2.
cresc.
cresc.
1. Tromp. in C.
2. u. 3. Tromp. in Es.
cresc.
cresc.
poco a poco cresc.
poco a poco cresc.
poco a poco cresc.
poco a poco cresc.
poco a poco cresc.

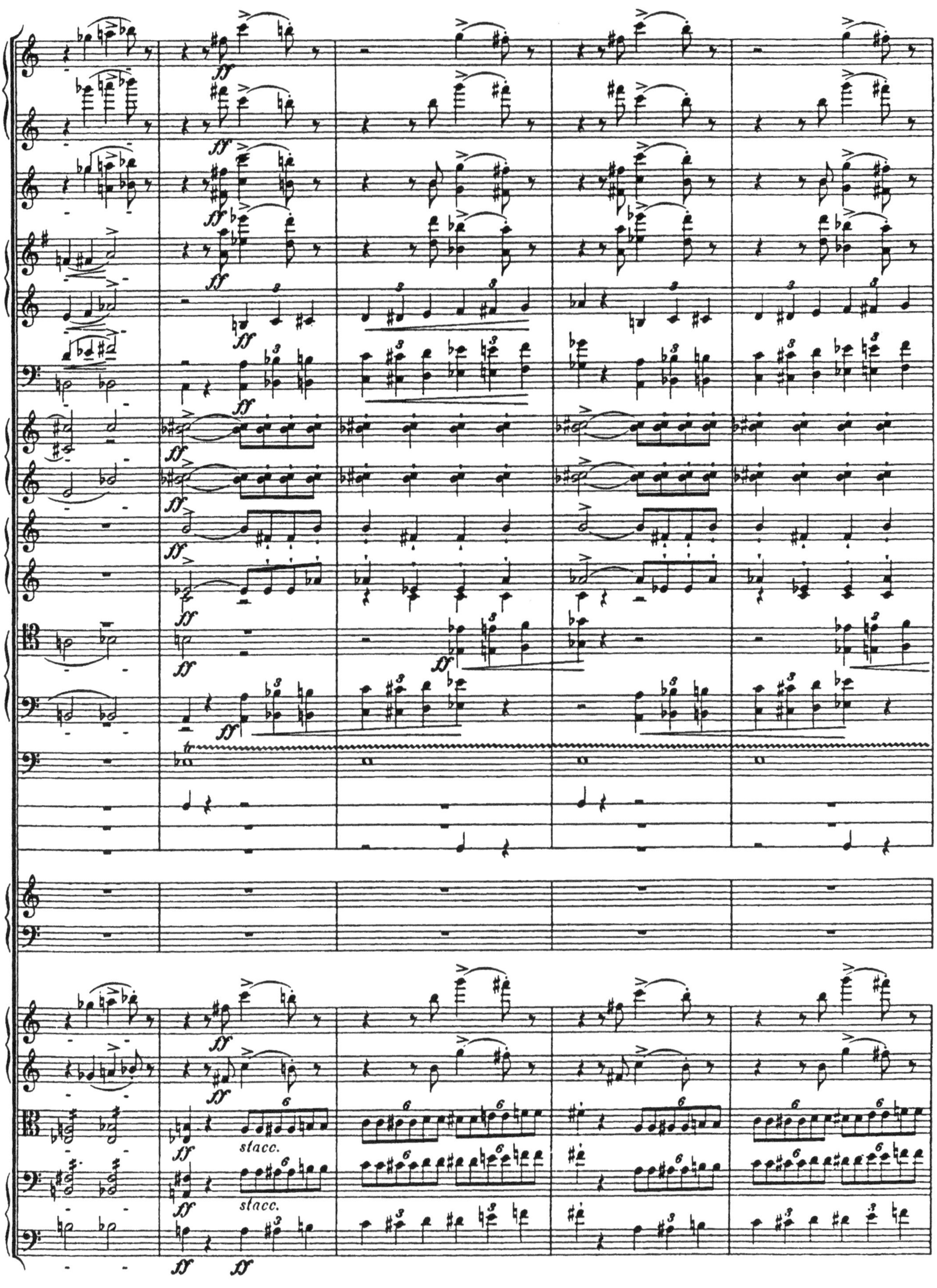
stacc.
stacc.

V
a 2.
sempre ff
a 2.
sempre ff
sempre ff
a 2.
sempre ff
sempre ff
sempre ff
sempre ff
sempre ff
sempre ff
sempre ff
V

sempre ff
sempre ff
sempre ff
sempre ff
glissando
8
ff
sf
8
ff
sf

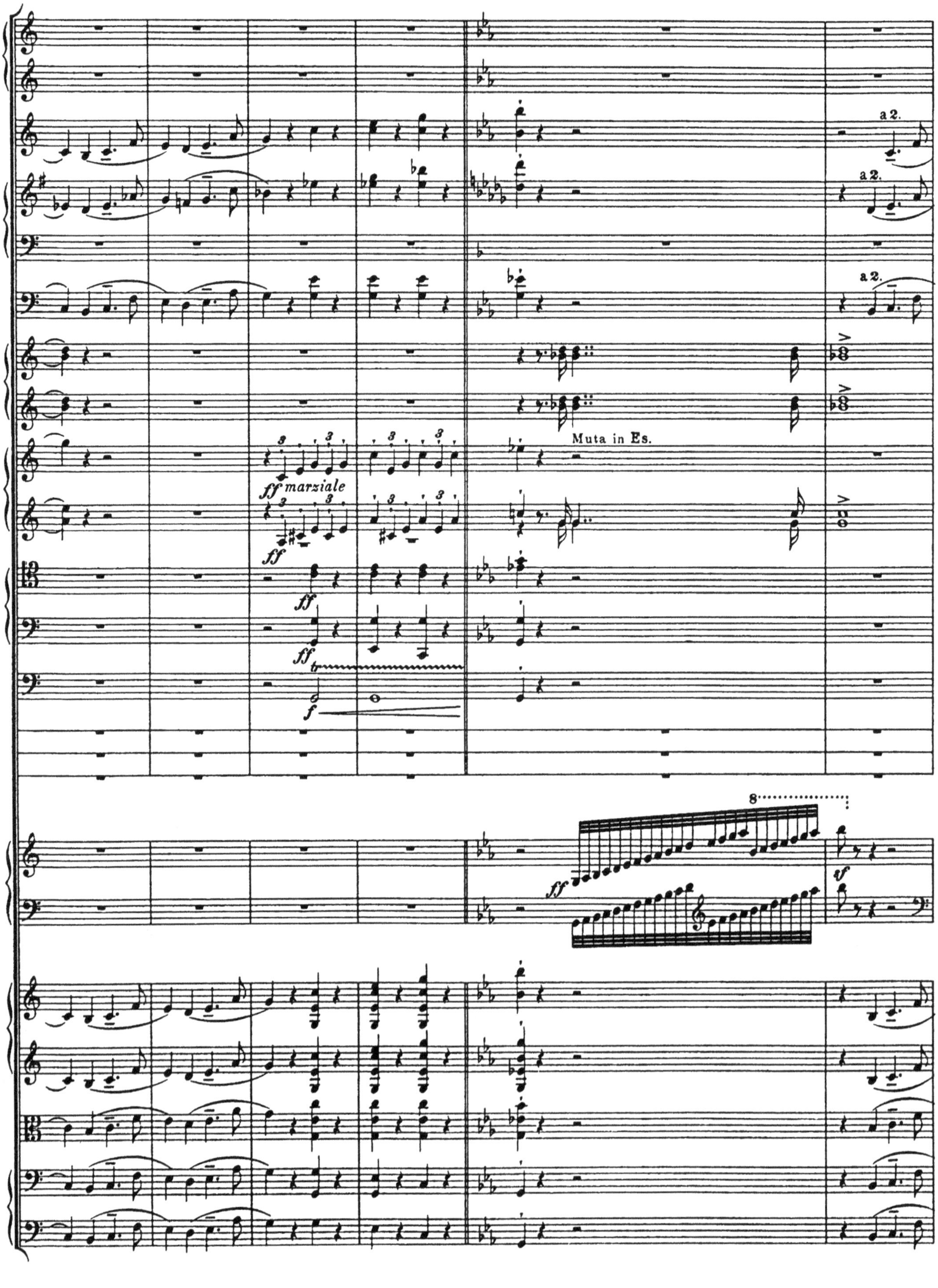
a 2.
a 2.
a 2.
Muta in Es.
ff marziale
ff
ff
ff
f
ff
ff
sf
8

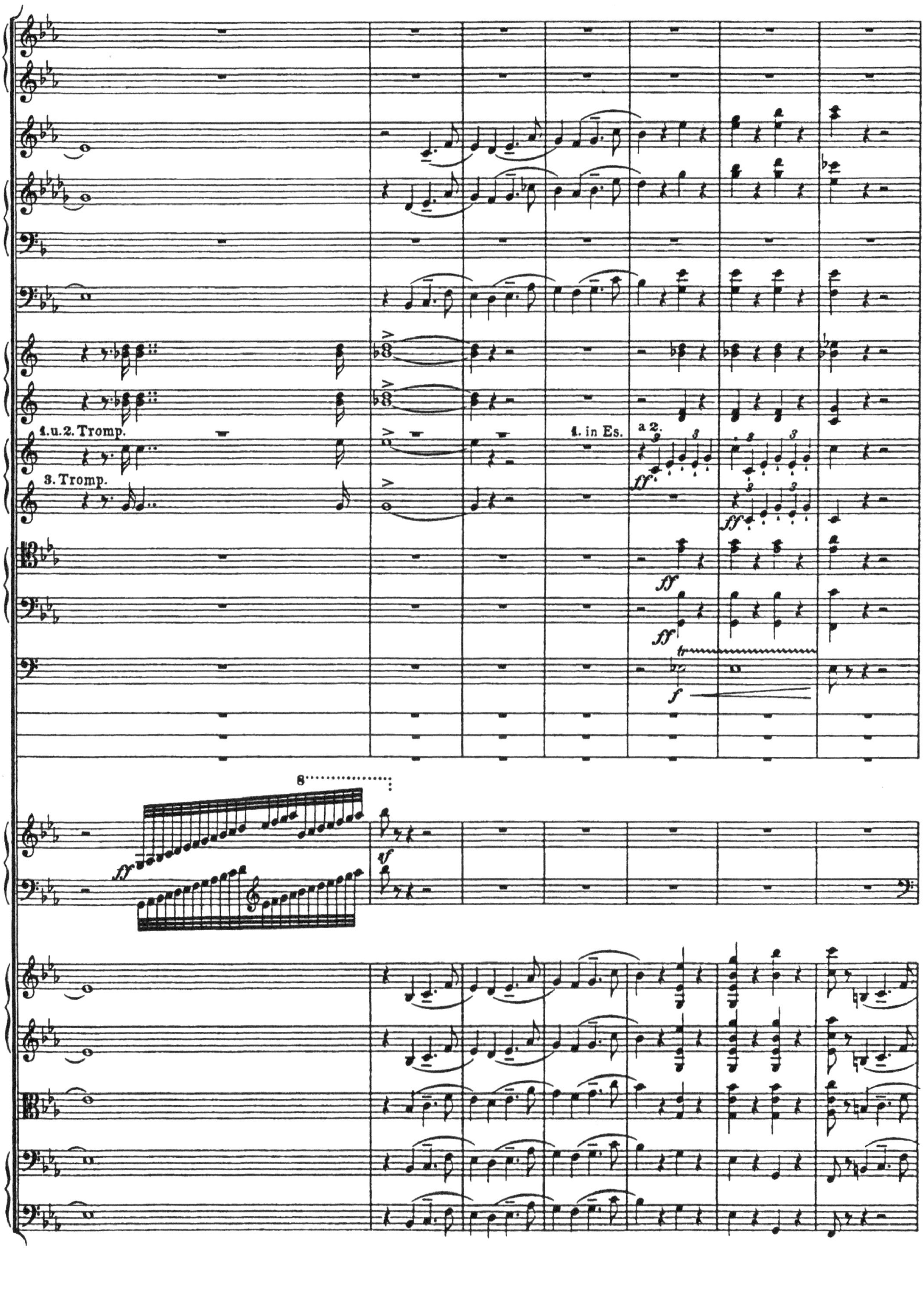
1.u.2. Tromp.
3. Tromp.
1. in Es.
a 2.
ff
f
tr
8
sf

108

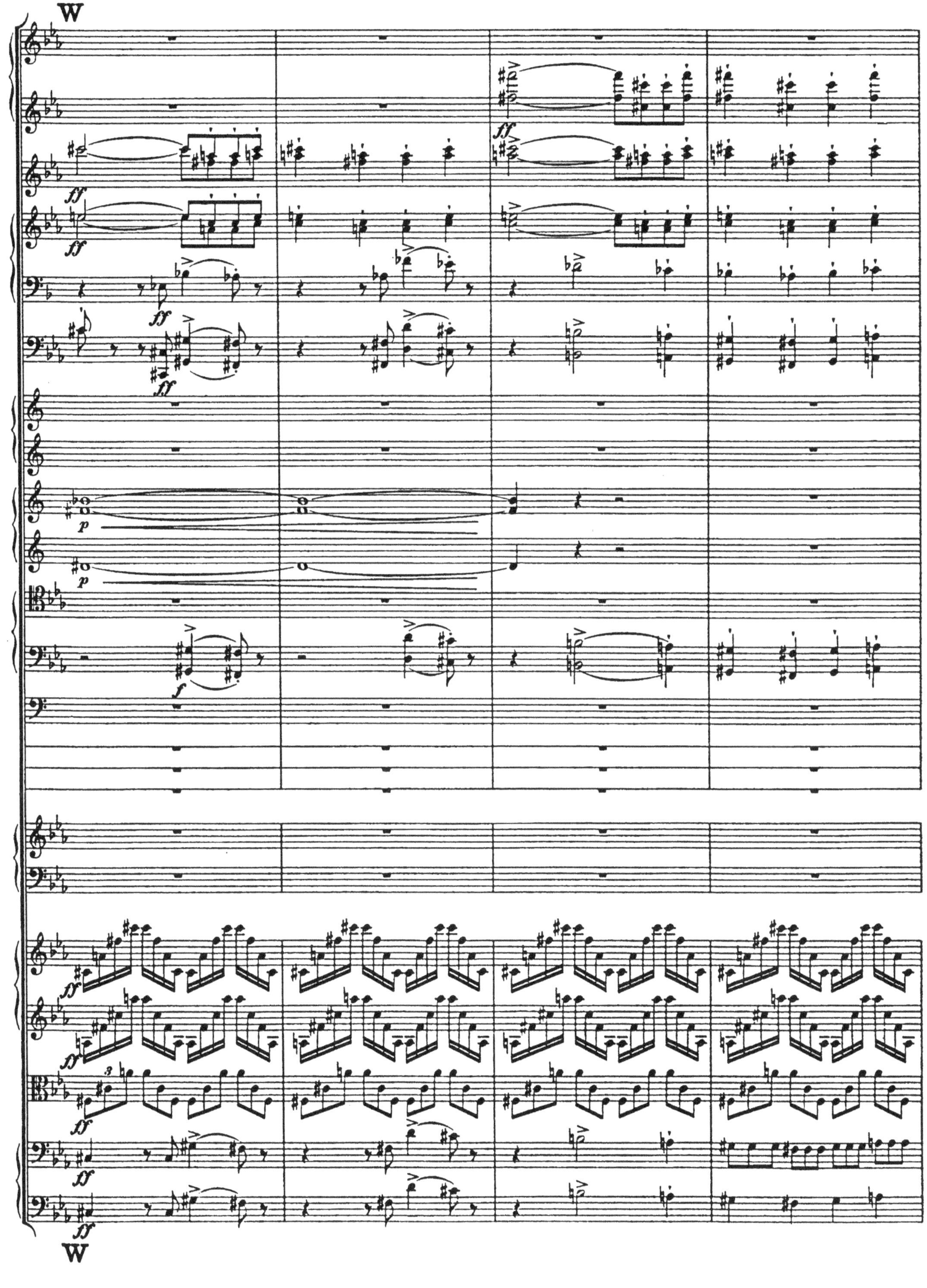
W
ff
p
f
3
W

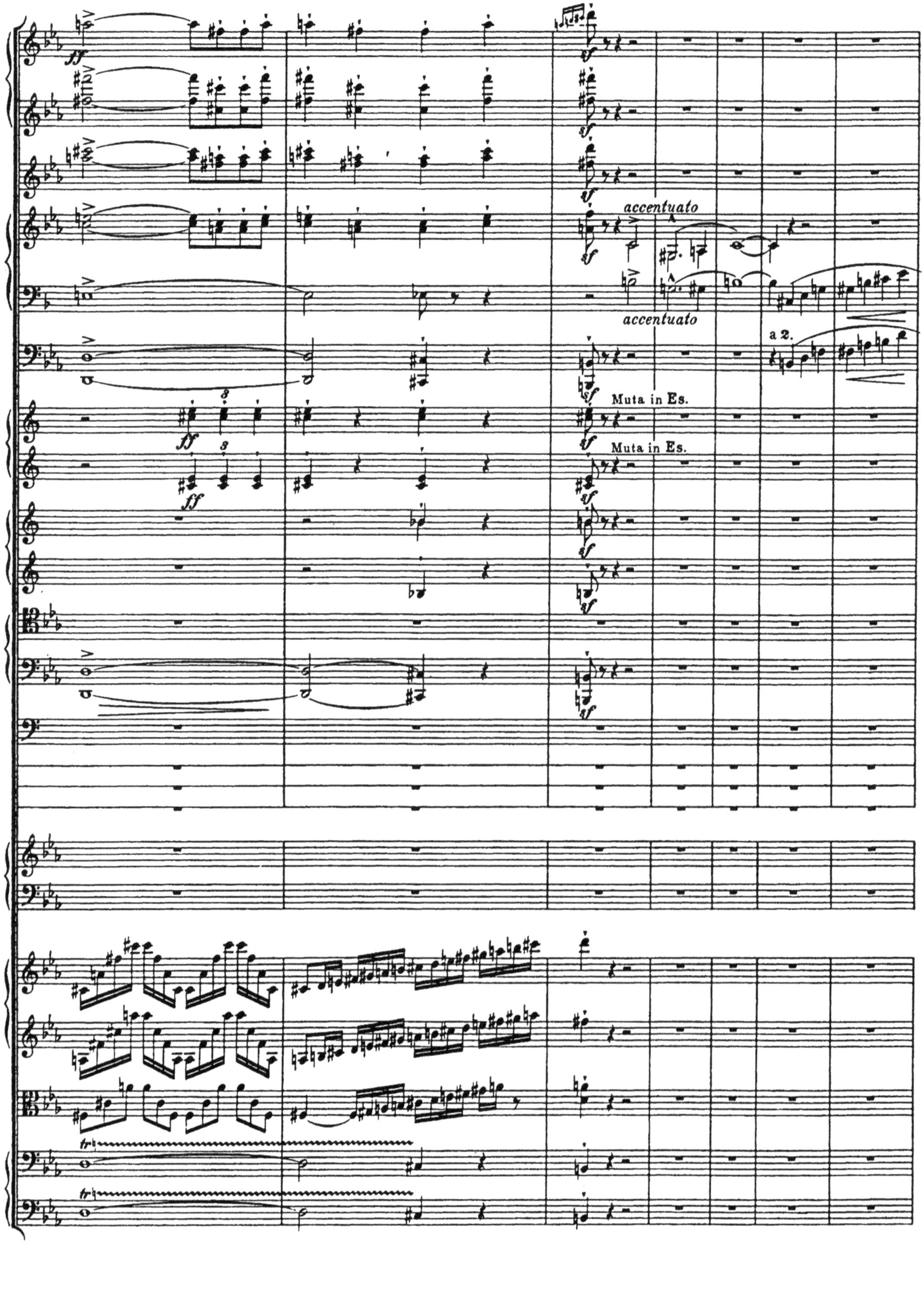
ff
sf
accentuato
accentuato
a 2.
Muta in Es.
Muta in Es.
ff
ff
tr

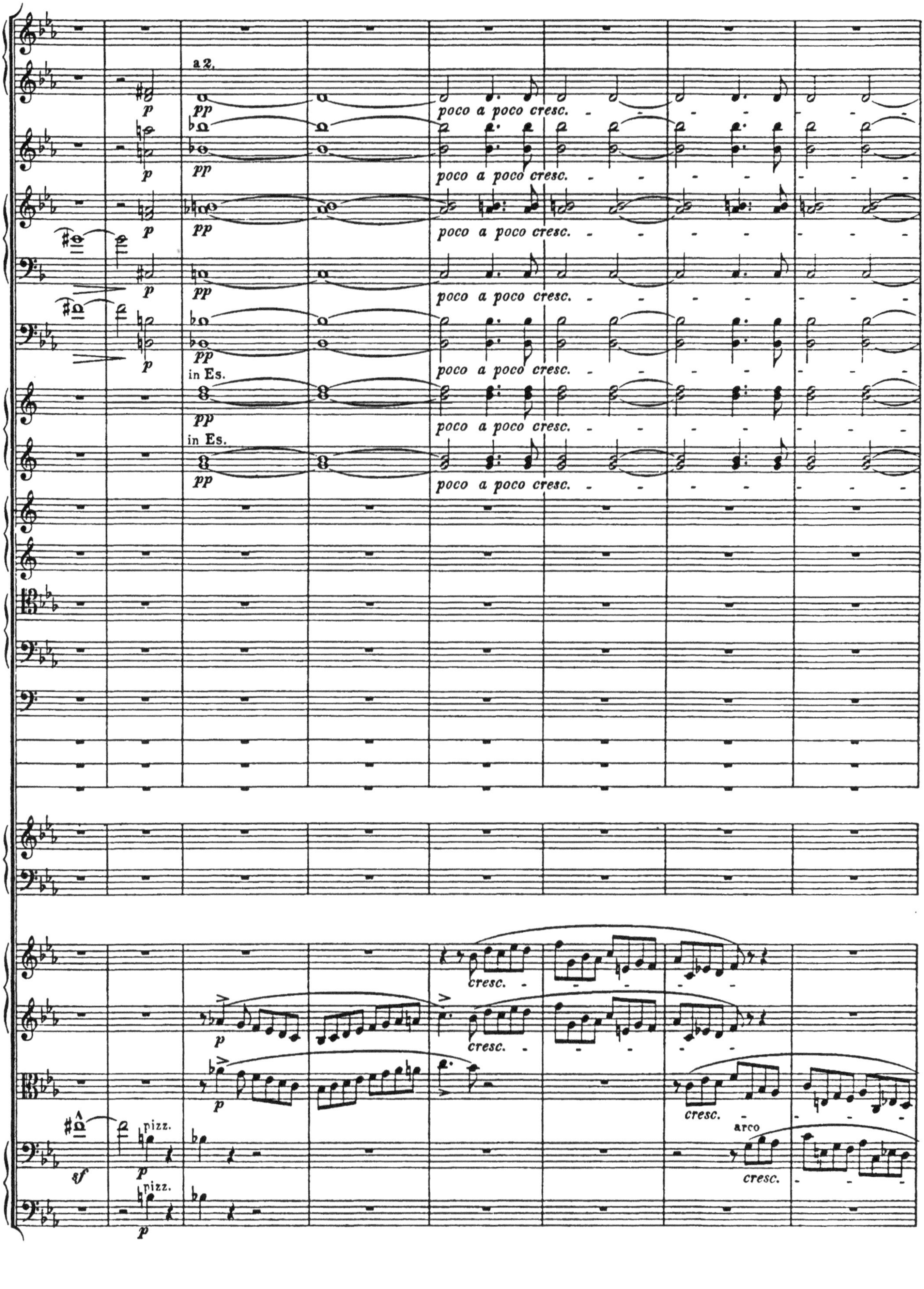
a 2.
p
pp
poco a poco cresc.
in Es.
in Es.
cresc.
sf
pizz.
pizz.
arco

X

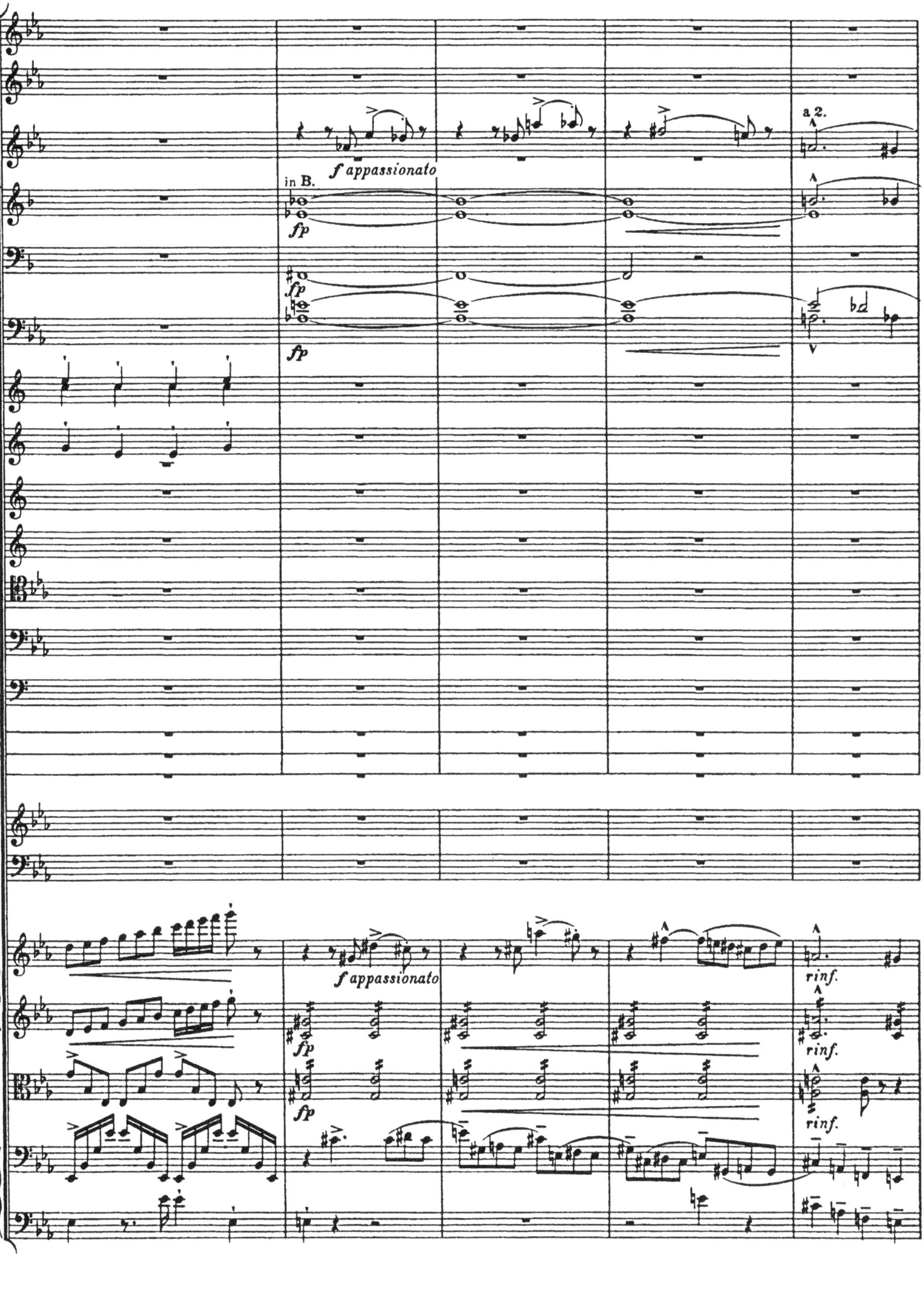
f appassionato
in B.
fp
a 2.
f appassionato
rinf.

f appassionato
fp
fp
fp
ff
ff
brillante
ff
brillante
ff
f appassionato
fp
ff
fp
ff
ff

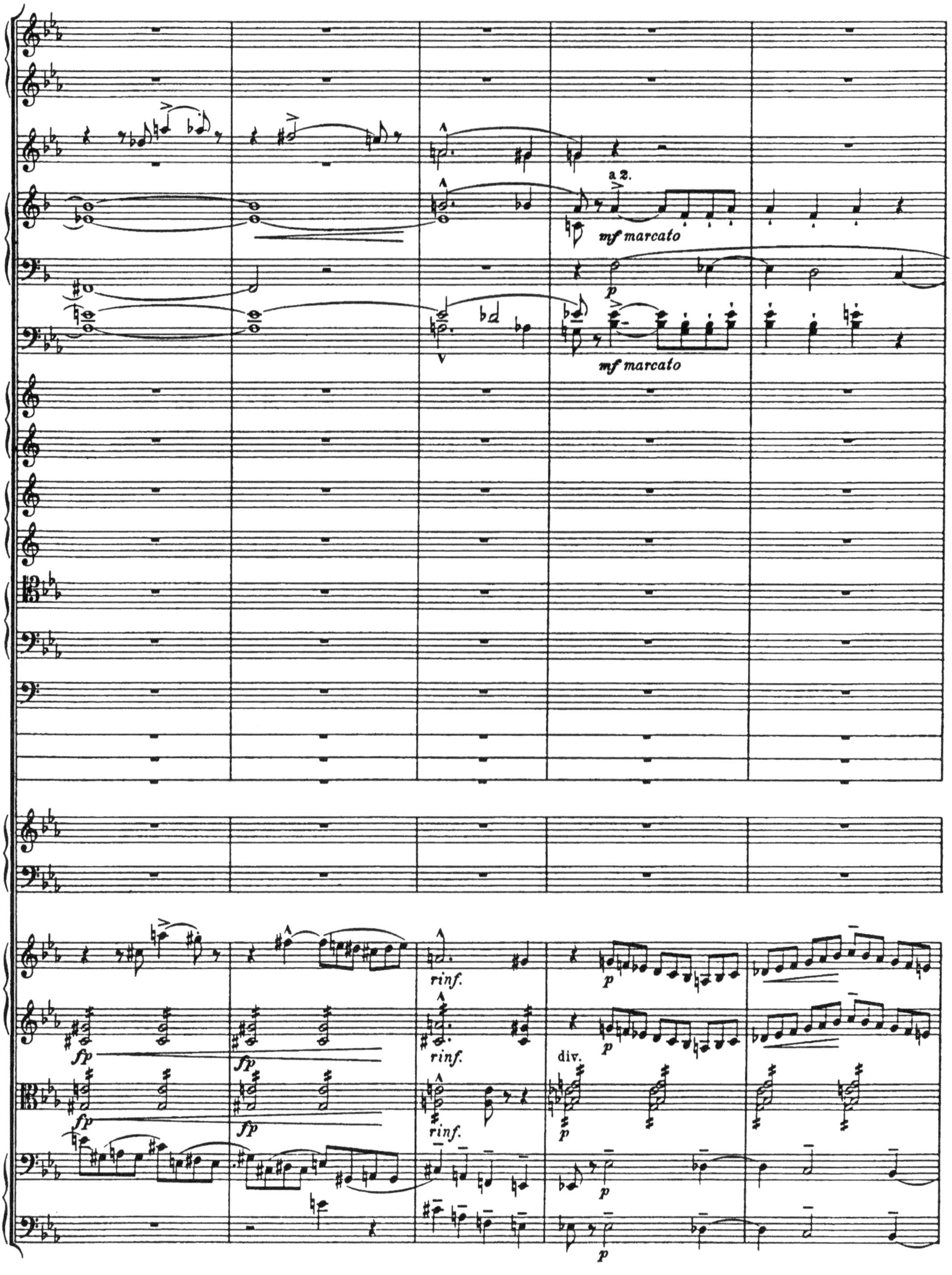
a 2.
mf marcato
p
mf marcato
rinf.
p
fp
rinf.
div.
fp
fp
rinf.
fp
p
p
p

116

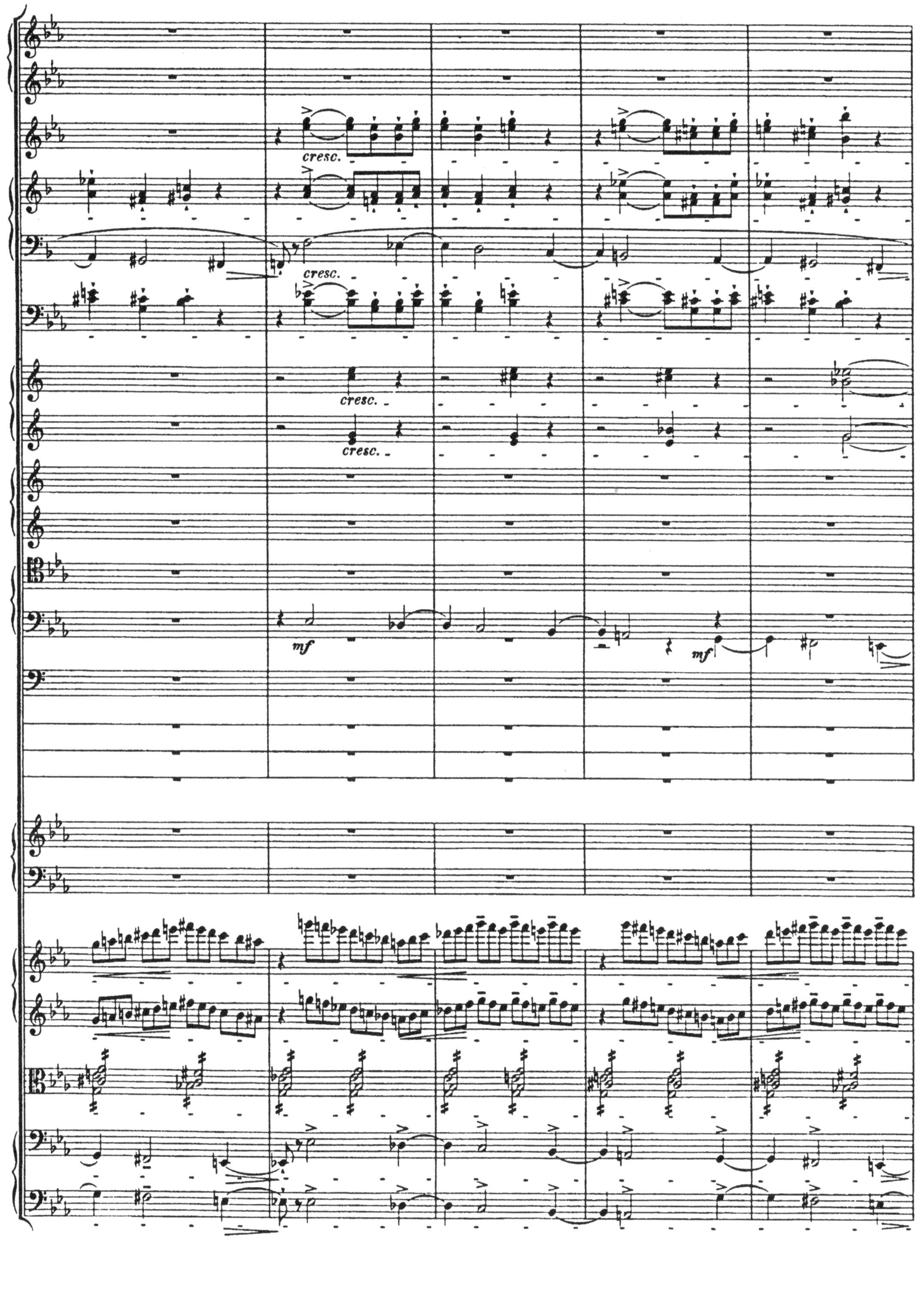
cresc.
cresc.
cresc.
cresc.
mf
mf

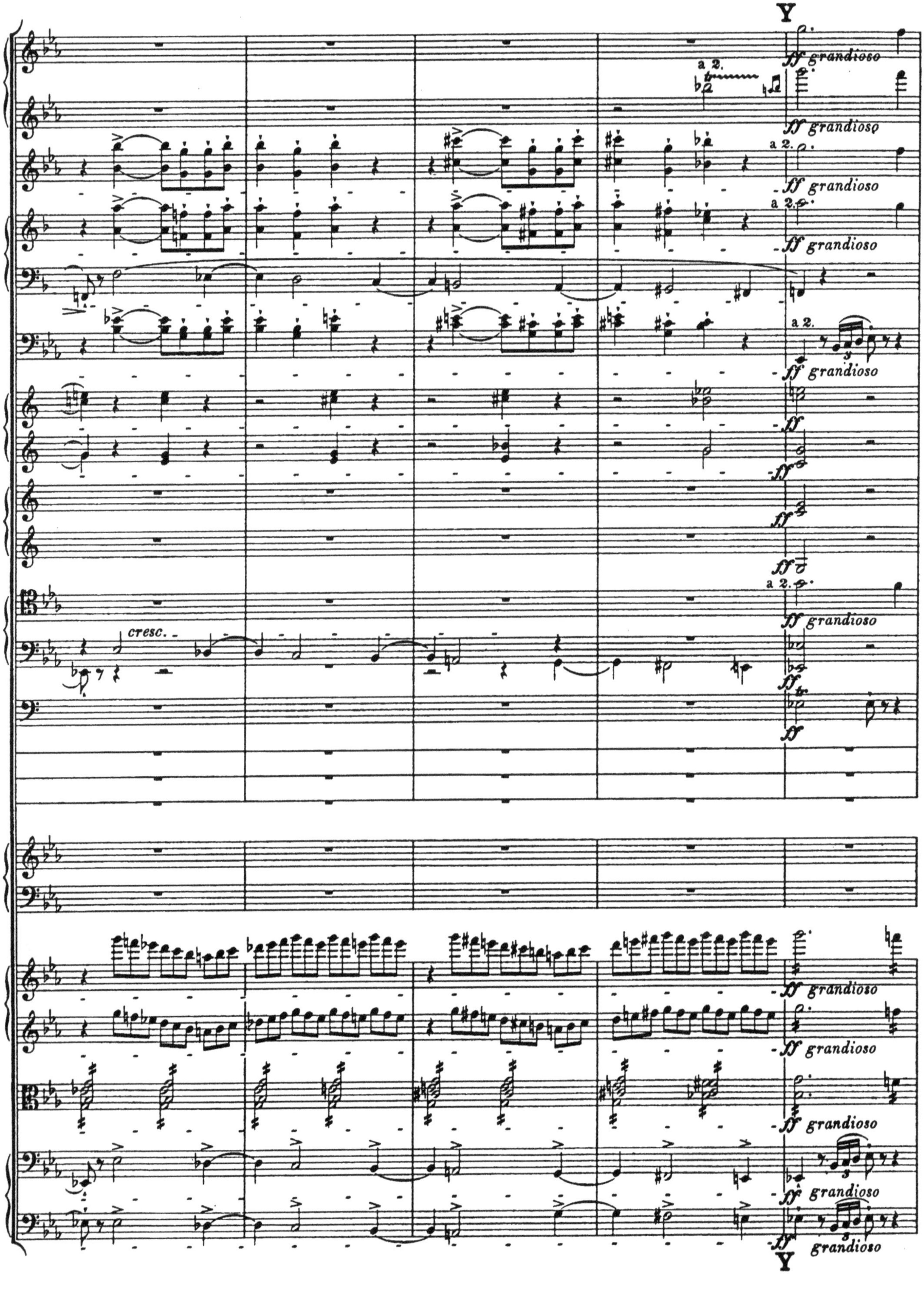
Y
a 2.
ff grandioso
cresc.
ff
Y

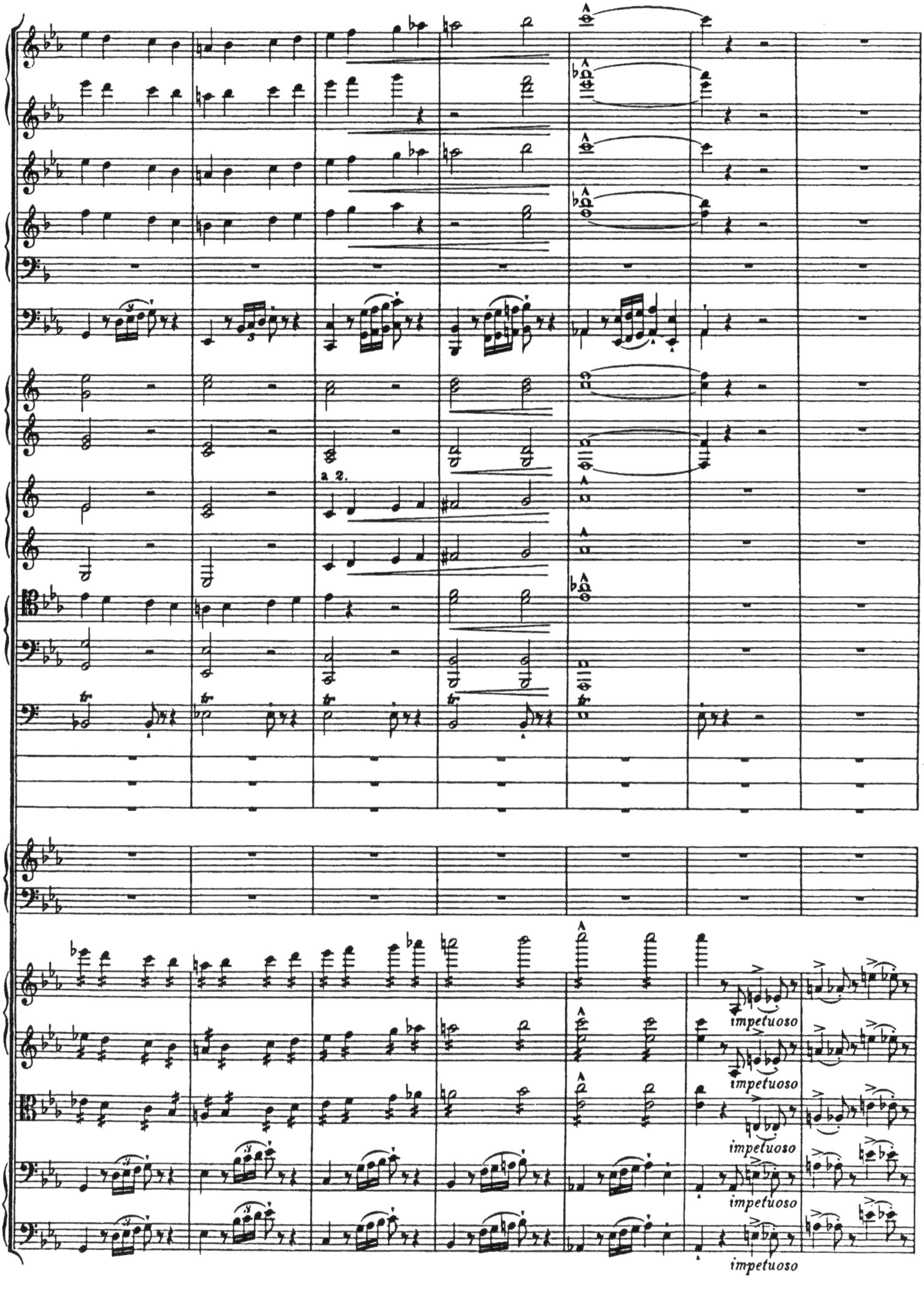
a 2.
impetuoso
impetuoso
impetuoso
impetuoso
impetuoso

a 2.
a 2.
tr
impetuoso
impetuoso
impetuoso
impetuoso
impetuoso

Z
un poco rallentando il tempo
sempre fff
a 2.
ff
stacc.
sempre fff
Z
un poco rallentando il tempo

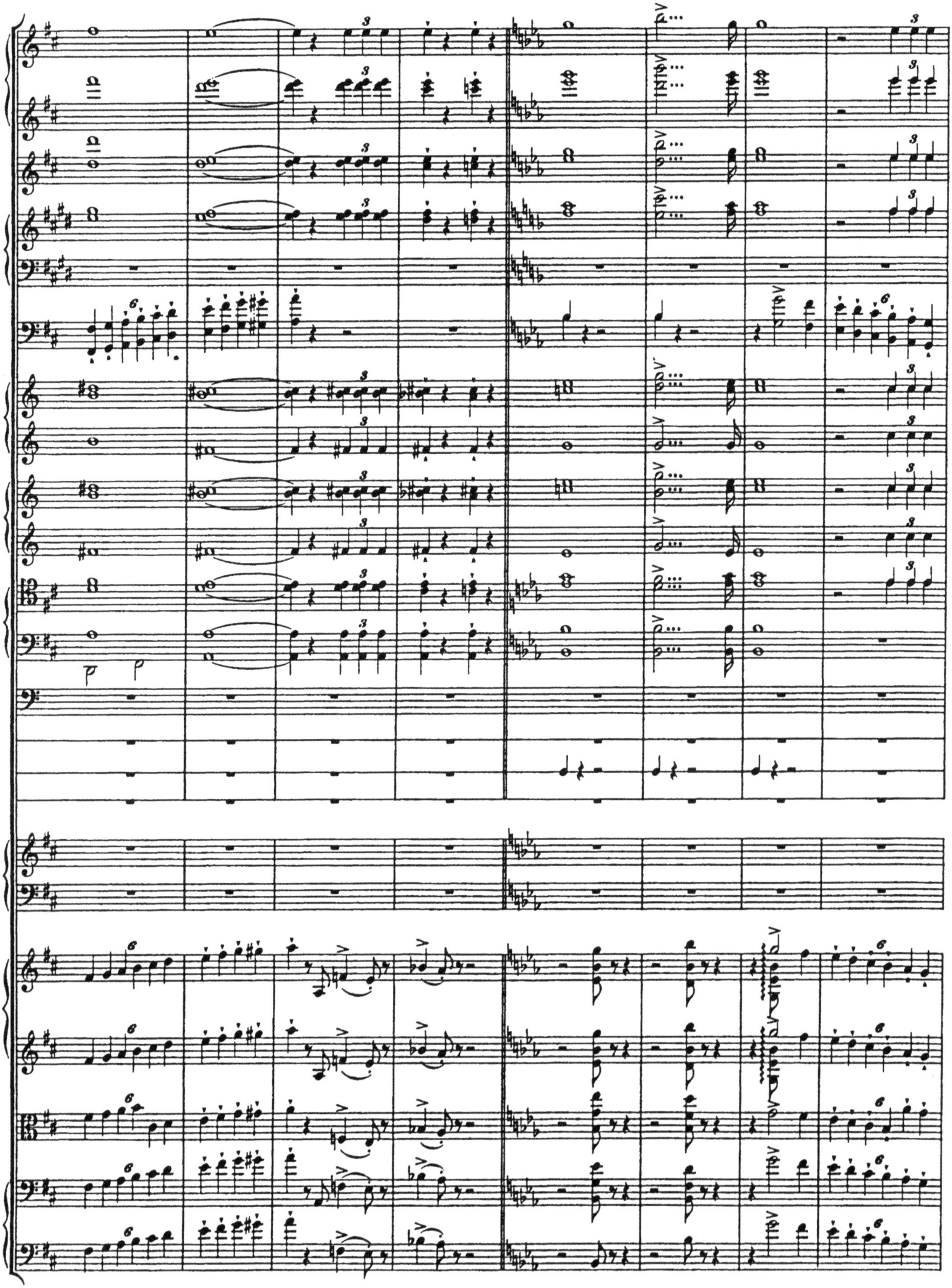
3
6
3
6
6
6
6

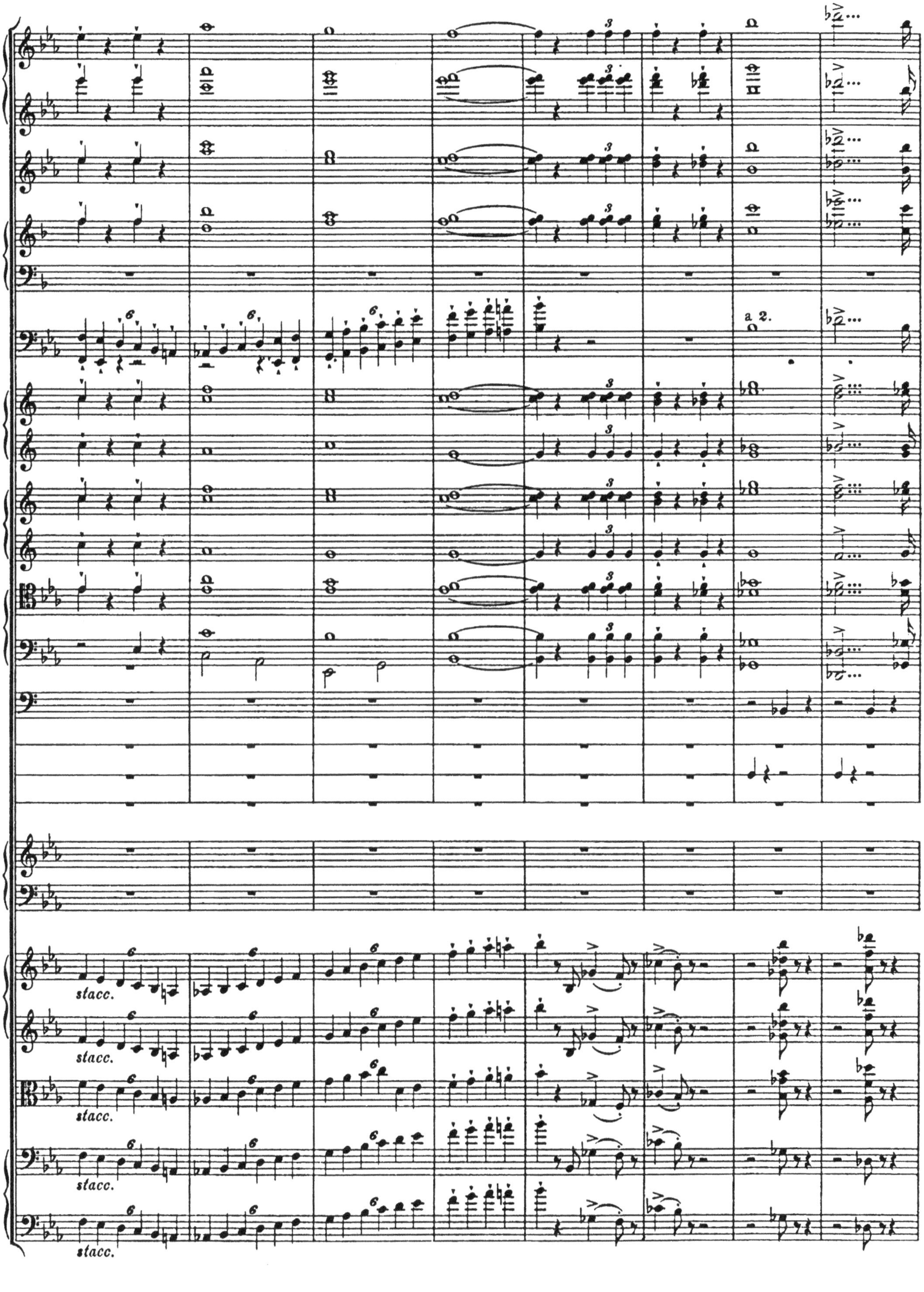
a 2.
stacc.
stacc.
stacc.
stacc.
stacc.

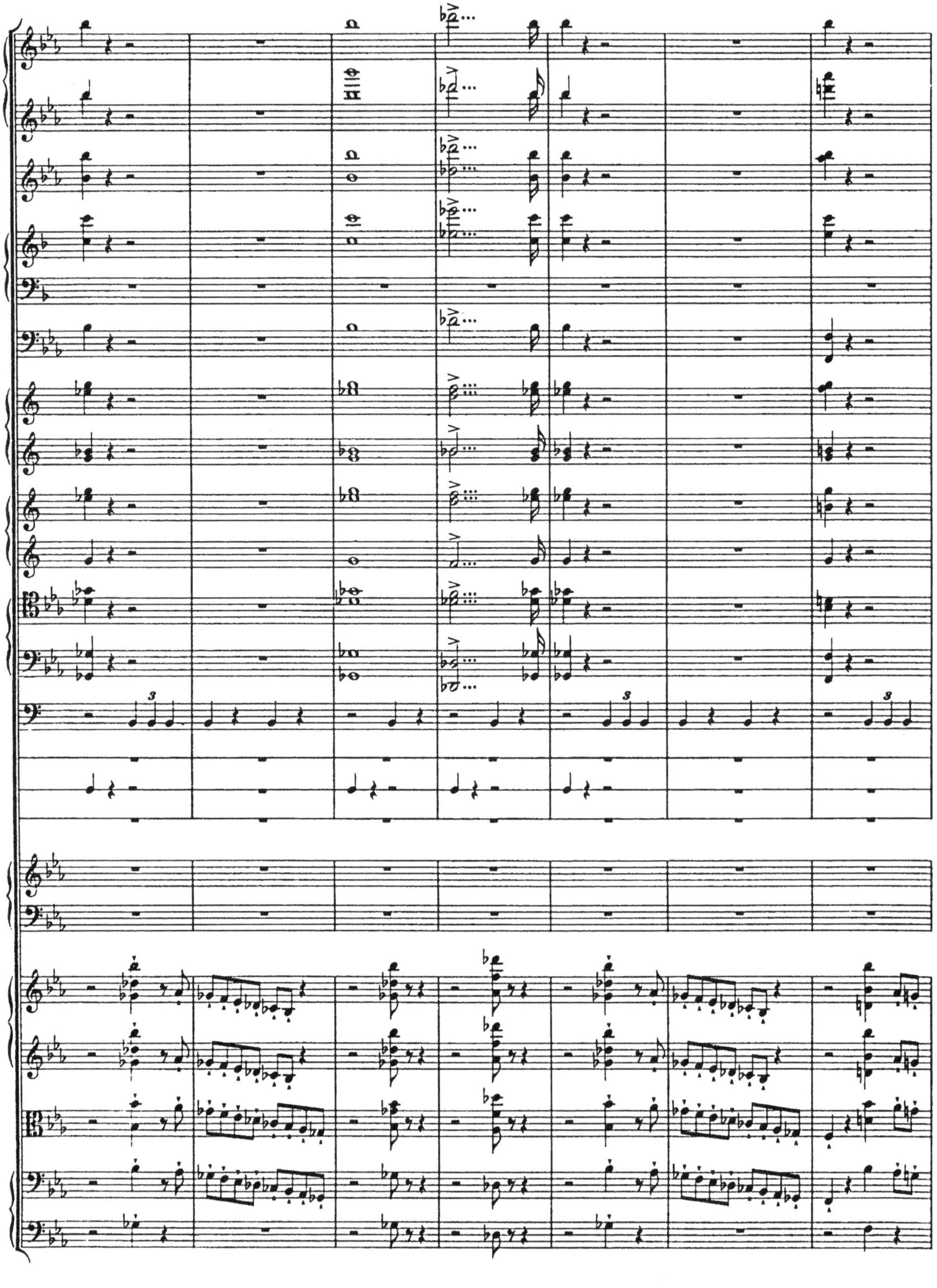

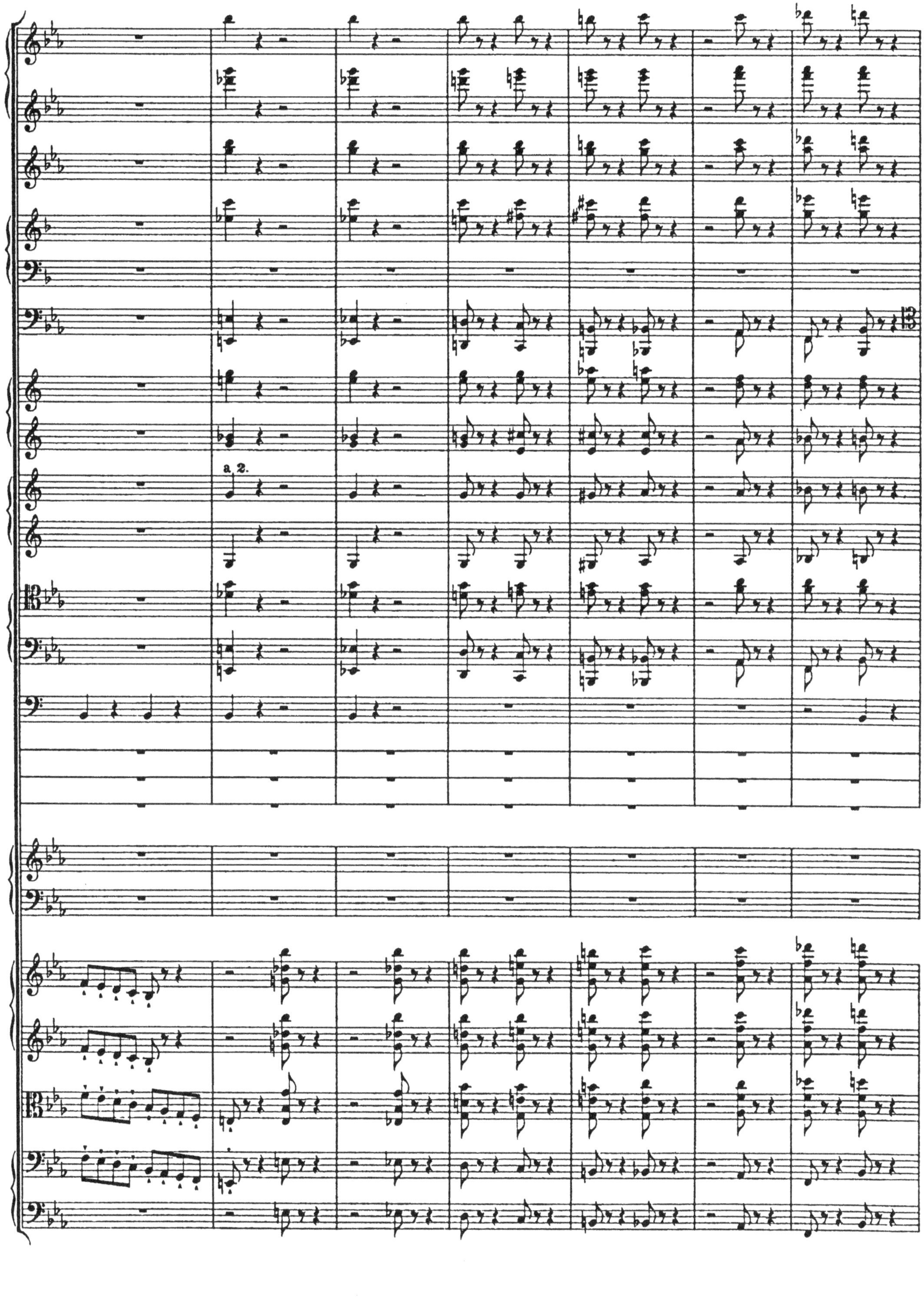
a 2.

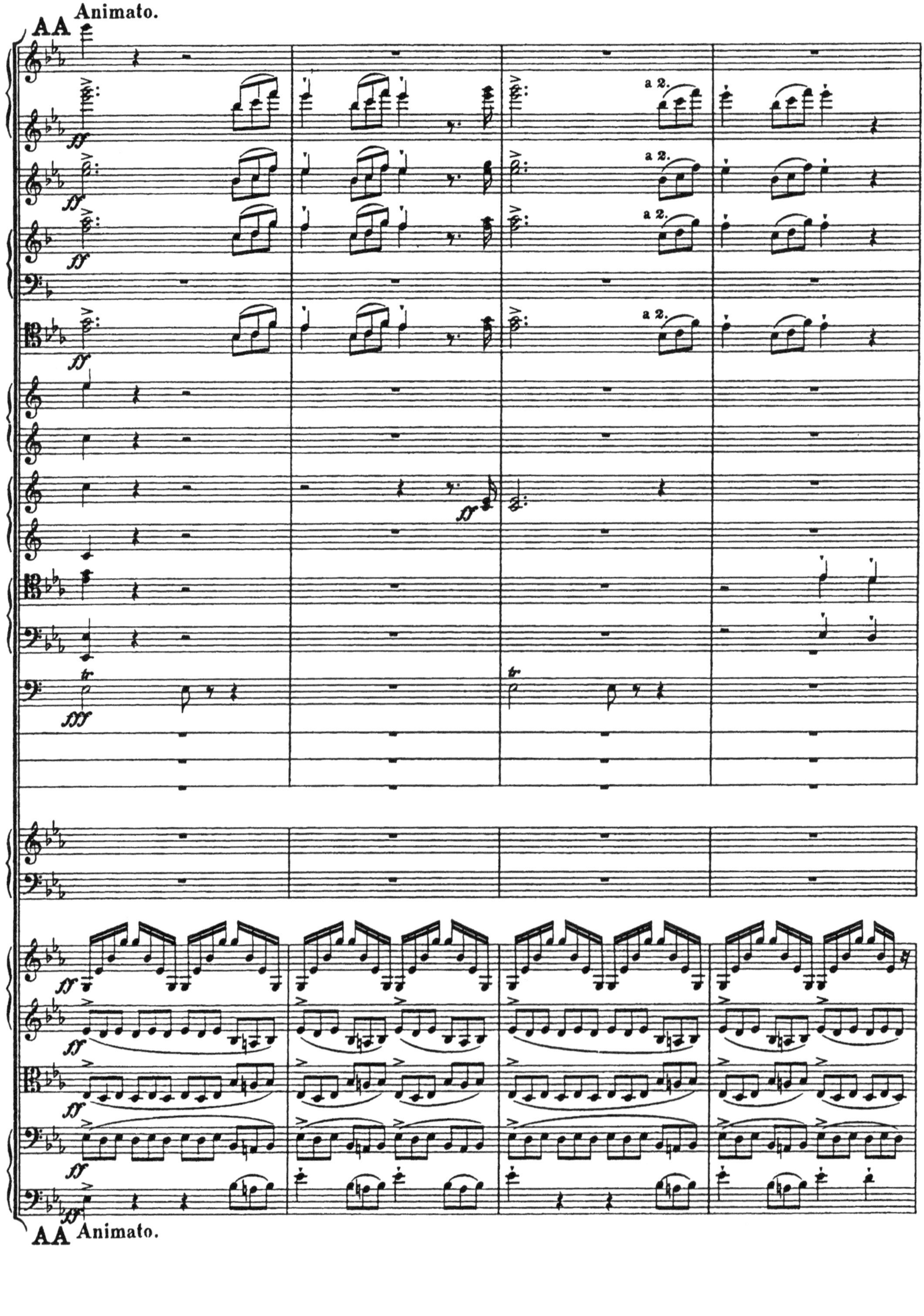
AA Animato.
a 2.
a 2.
a 2.
a 2.
AA Animato.

più cresc.
più cresc.
più cresc.
ff
più cresc.
p
più cresc.
p
più cresc.
sf
sf
marcato
p
molto cresc. e rinf.
p
molto cresc. e rinf.
p
molto cresc. e rinf.
marcato
rinf. molto
marcato
rinf. molto

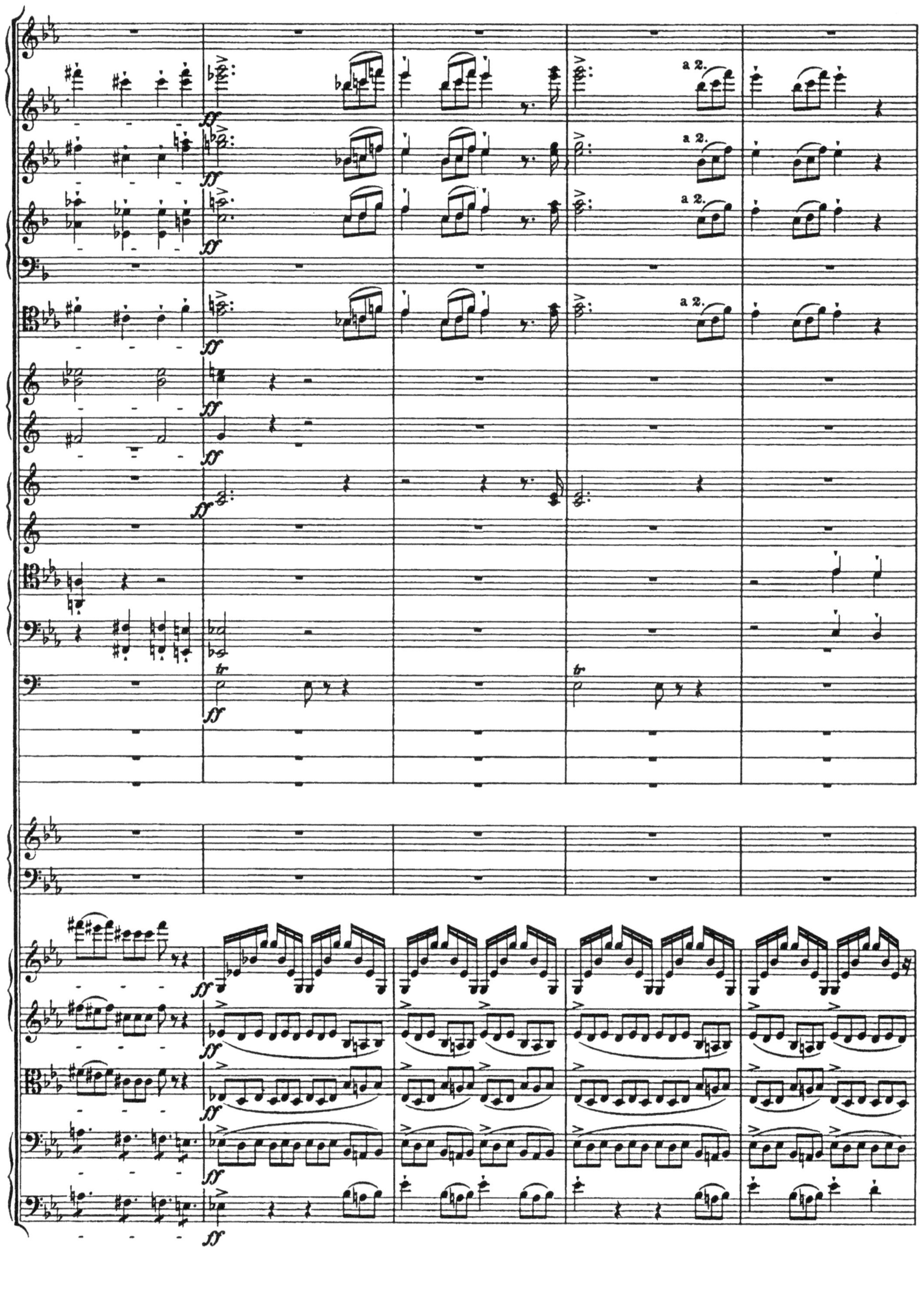
a 2.
a 2.
a 2.
a 2.
ff
tr

più cresc.
più cresc.
più cresc.
p
più cresc.
p
più cresc.
p
più cresc.
sf
sf
p
p
molto cresc. e rinf.
p
molto cresc. e rinf.
p
molto cresc. e rinf.
marcato
rinf. molto
marcato
rinf. molto

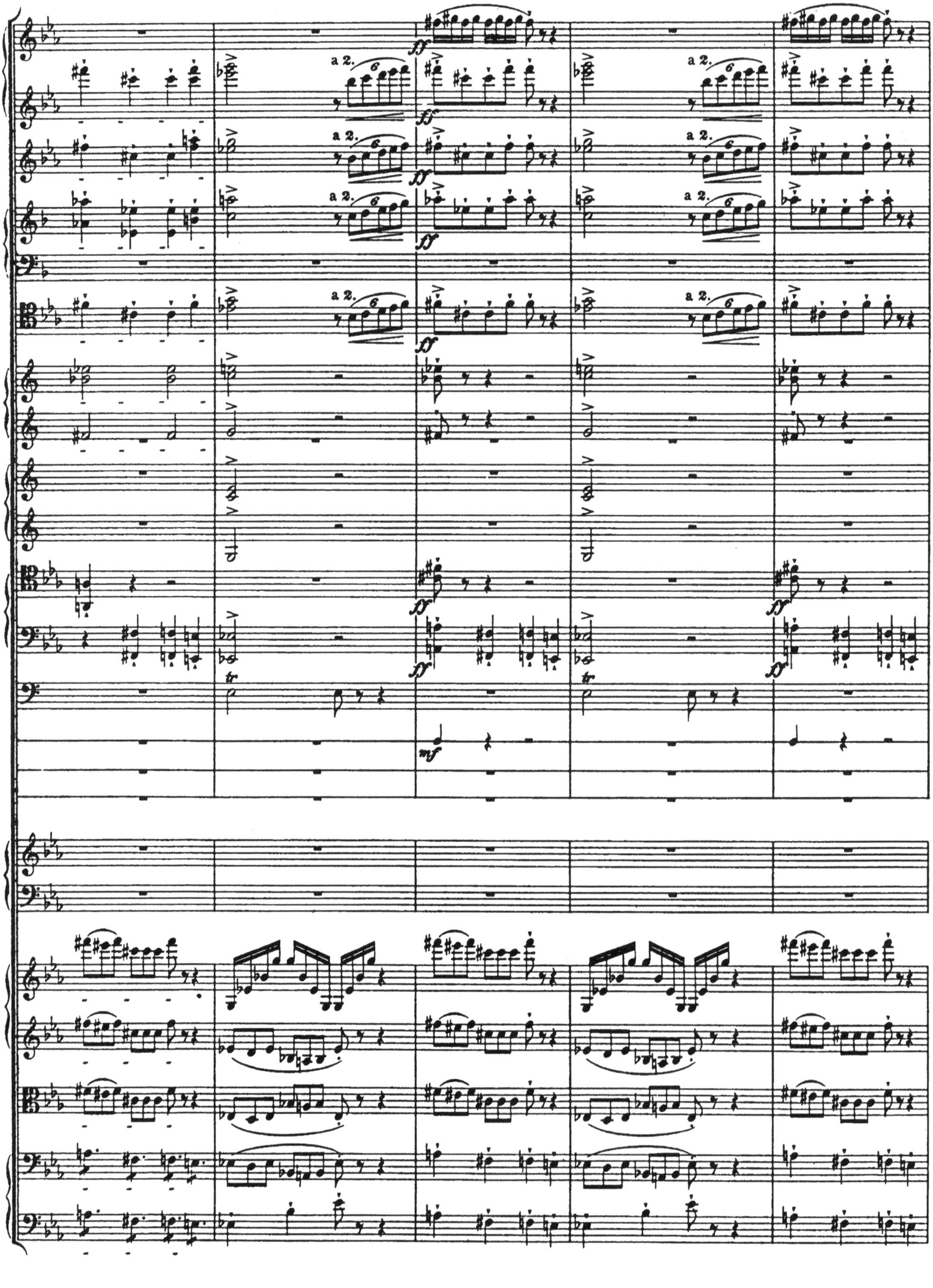
a 2.
ff
tr
mf

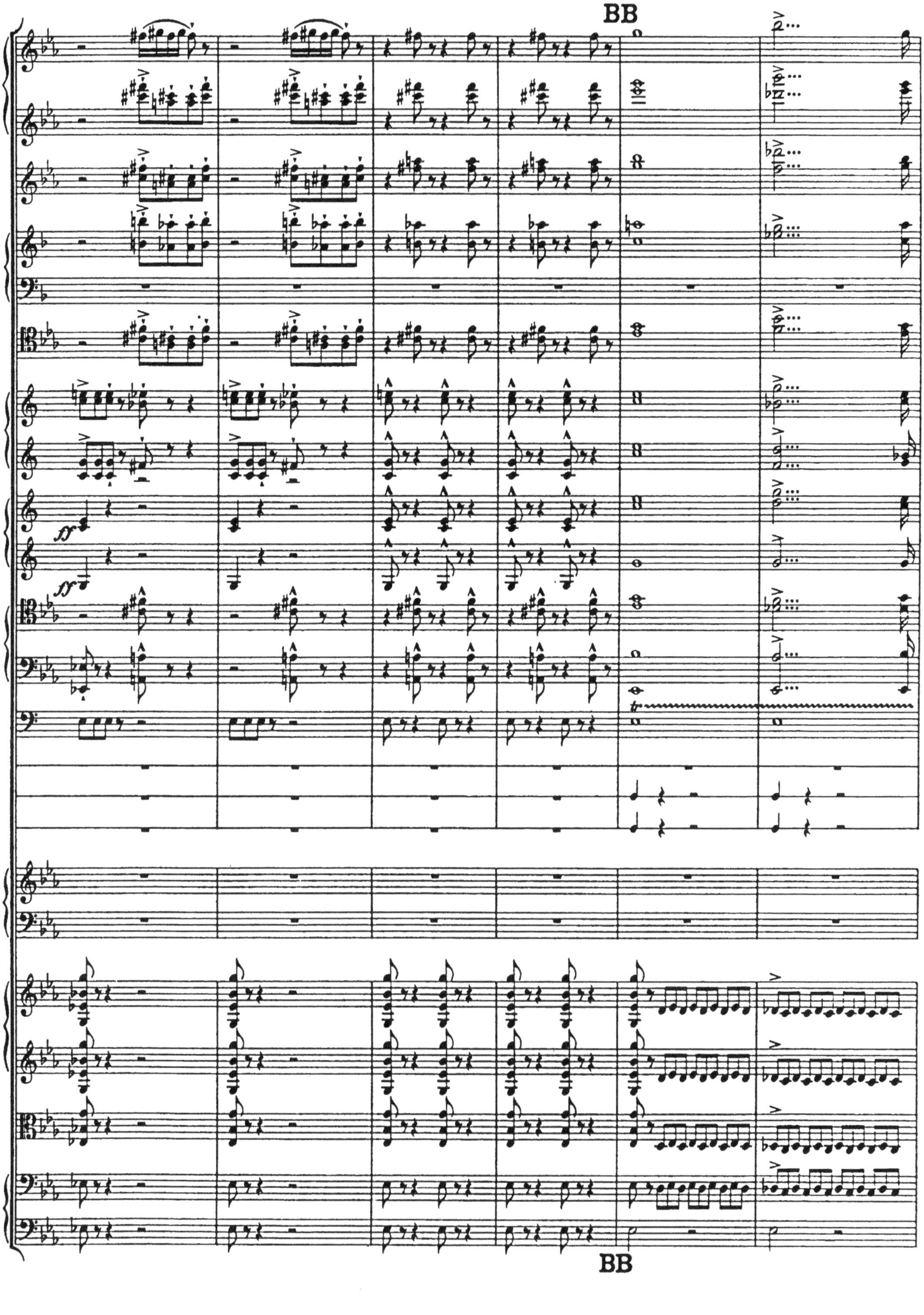
BB
ff
ff
BB

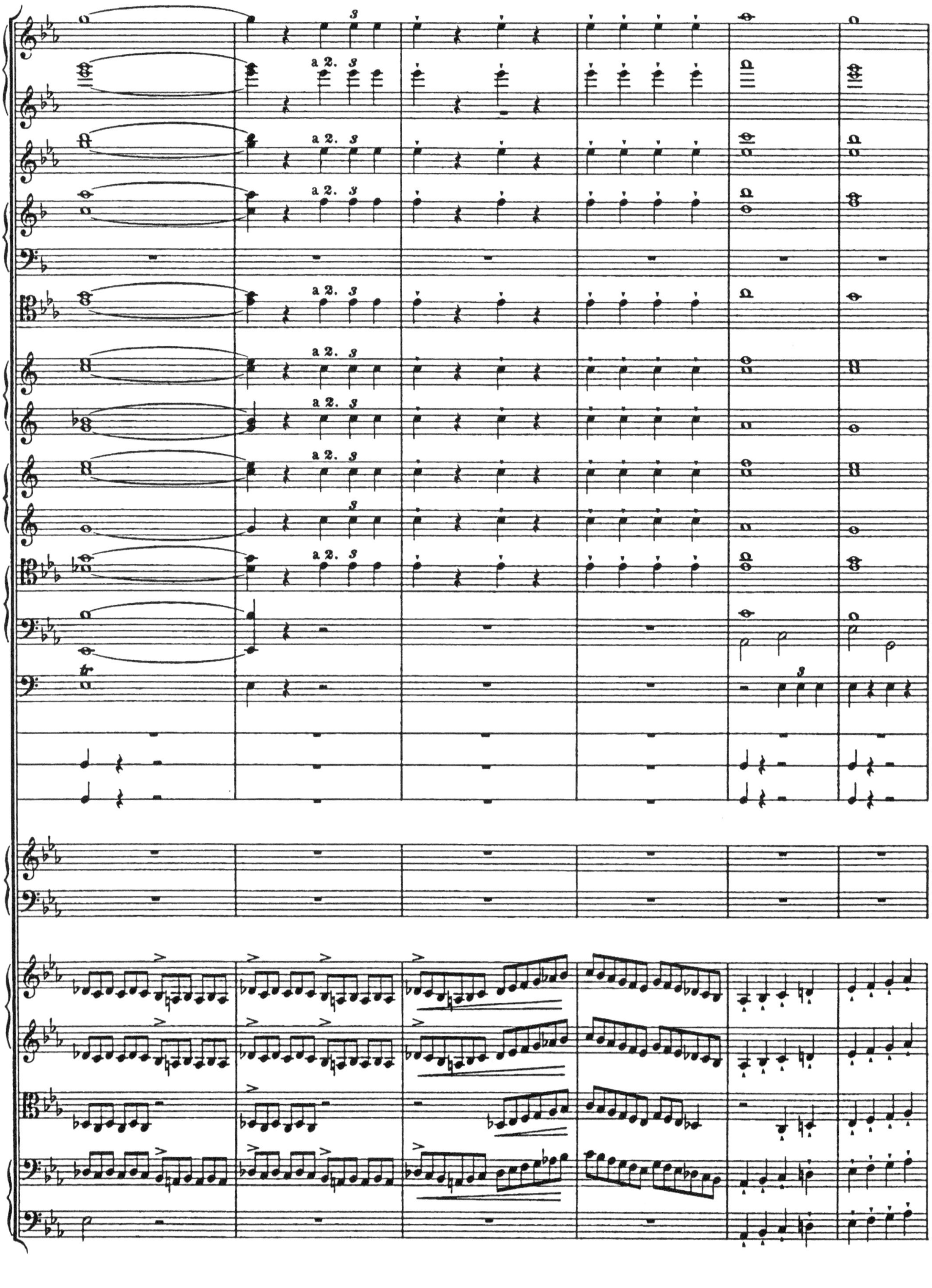
a 2.
3
tr

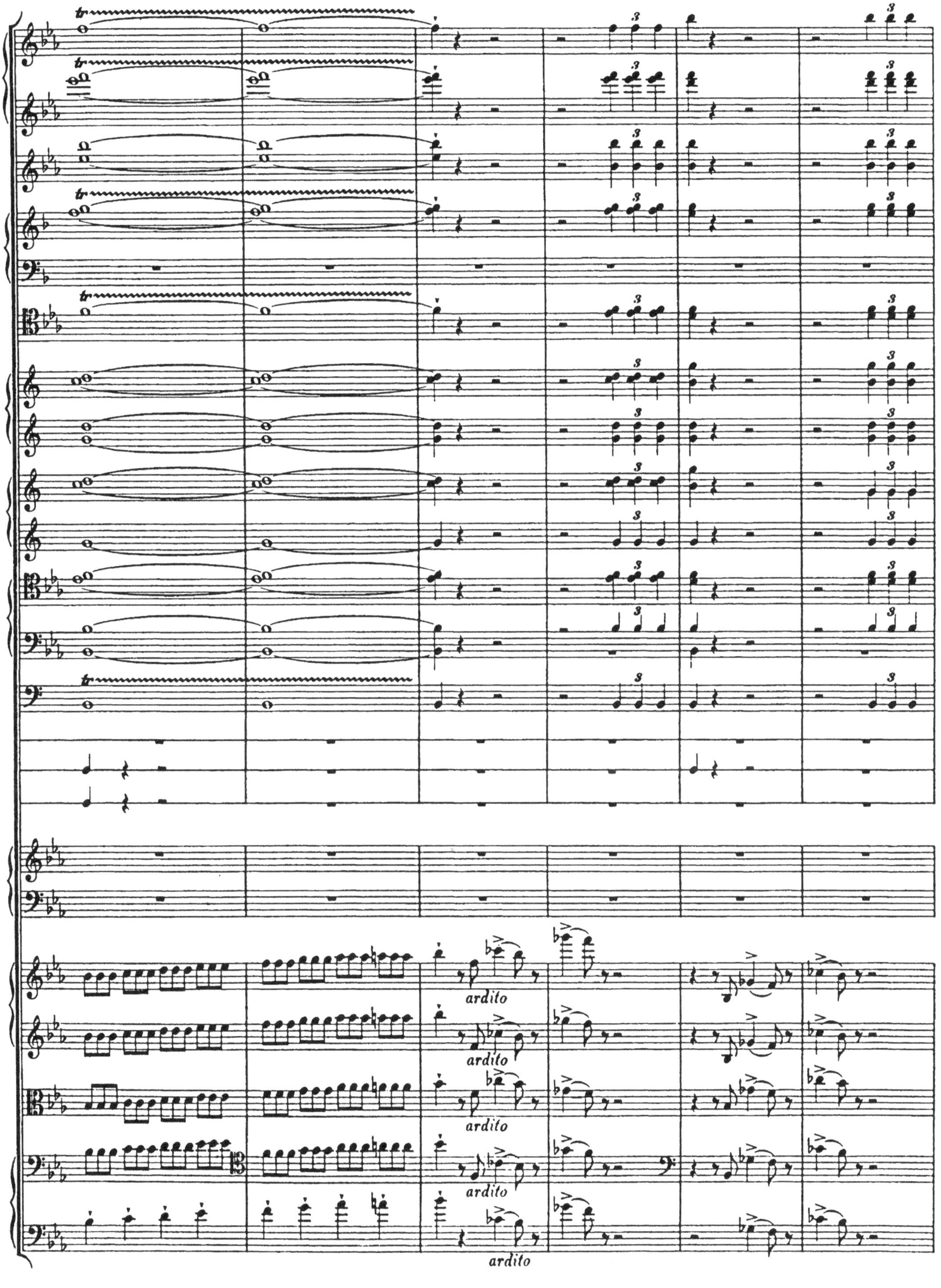
ardito
ardito
ardito
ardito
ardito

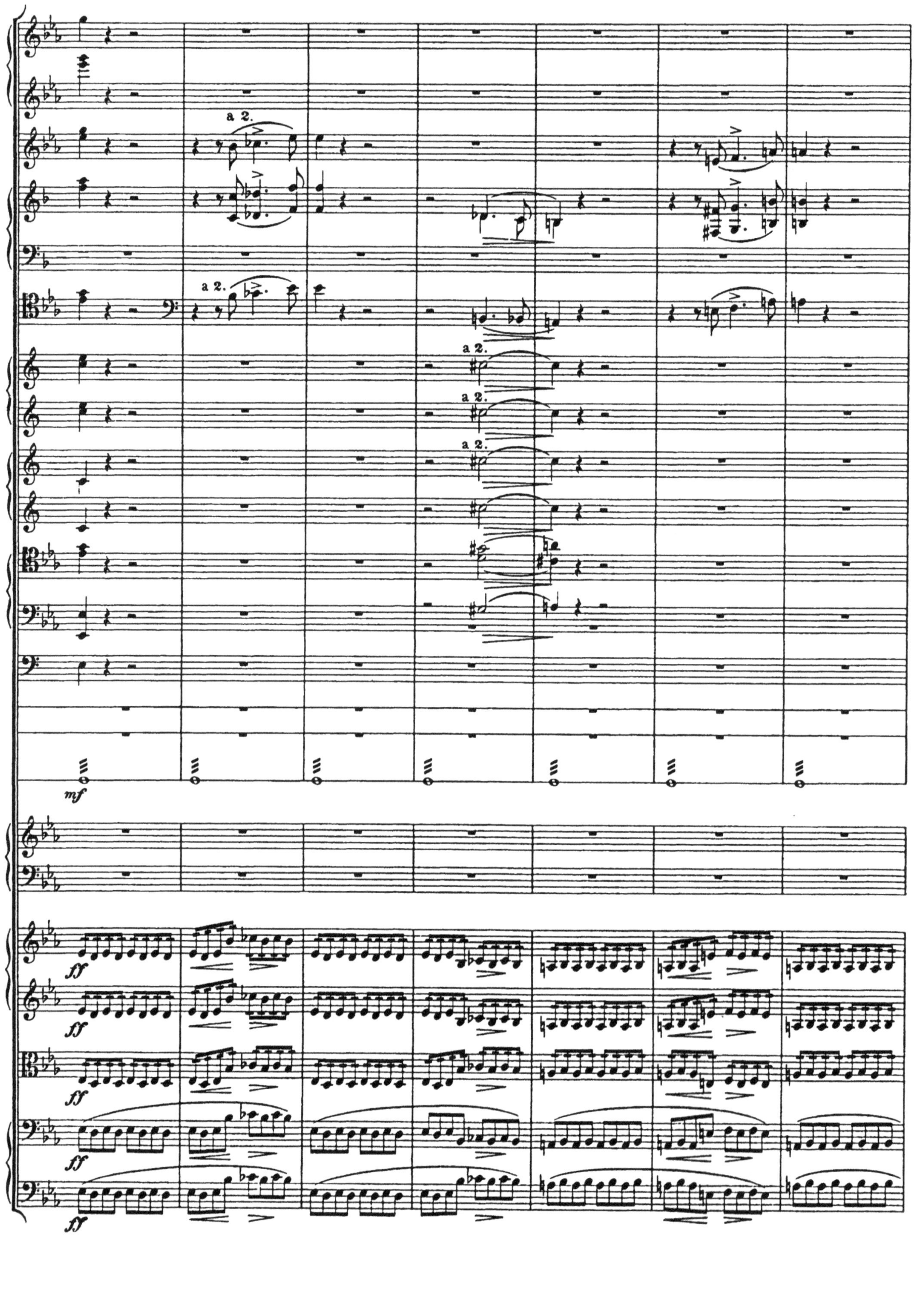
a 2.
a 2.
a 2.
a 2.
a 2.
mf
ff

a 2.
poco a poco dim.
poco a poco dim.
poco a poco dim.
poco a poco dim.
poco a poco dim.
poco a poco dim.

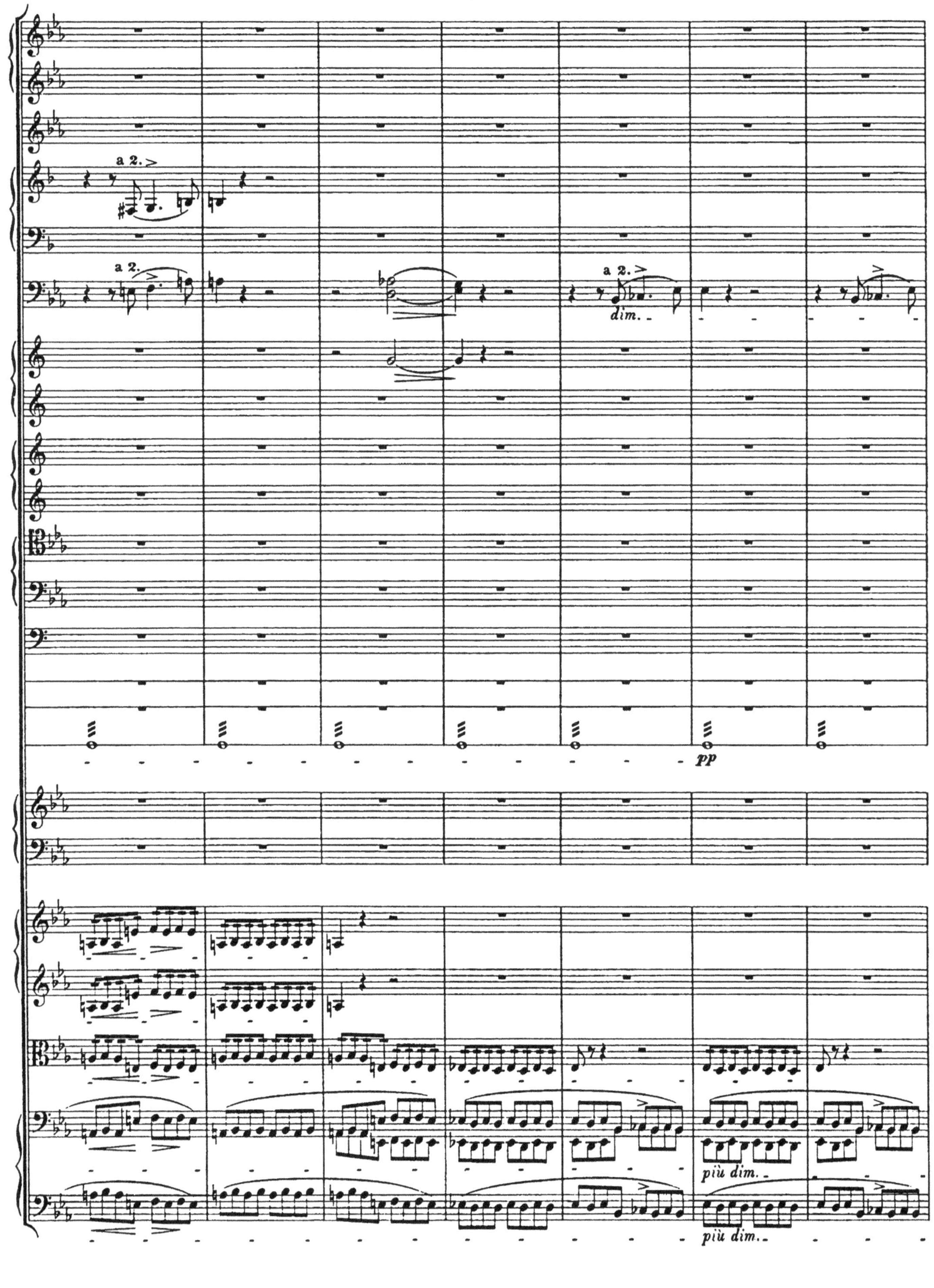
a 2.
a 2.
a 2.
dim.
pp
più dim.
più dim.

poco a poco rallentando
CC
dim.
p
pp
poco a poco rallentando
pp
CC

Più moderato.

rallentando
solenne
3
p
calmato
Bratschen.
calmato
rallentando

Andante religioso.

Andante religioso.

Violoncelle.

p dol. espressivo
p
p
p dol. espressivo
dol. espressivo
dol. espressivo
p
p

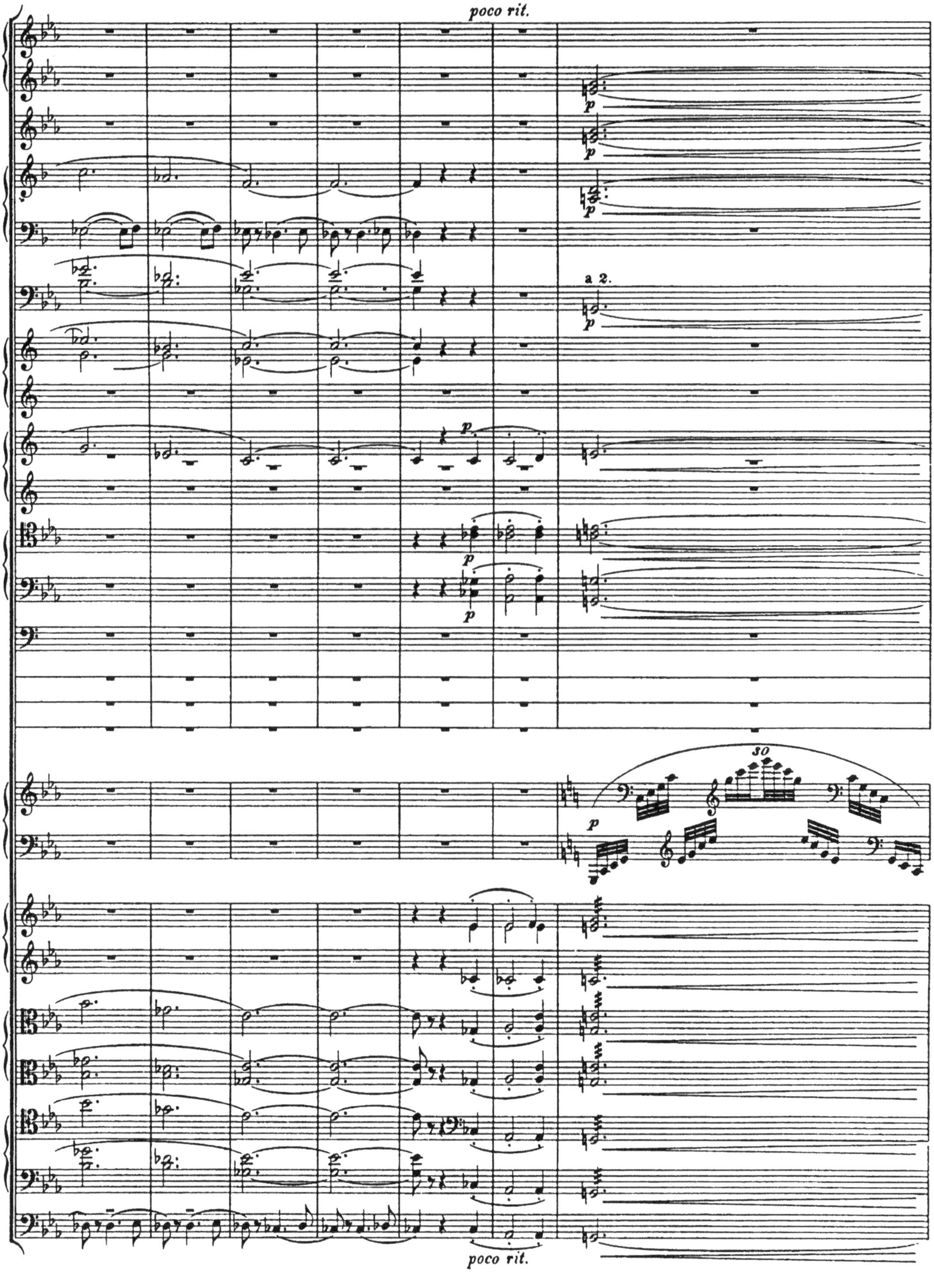
poco rit.
a 2.
p
30
poco rit.

Allegro moderato.

so

dim.

pizz.

pp

pizz.

pp

Allegro moderato.

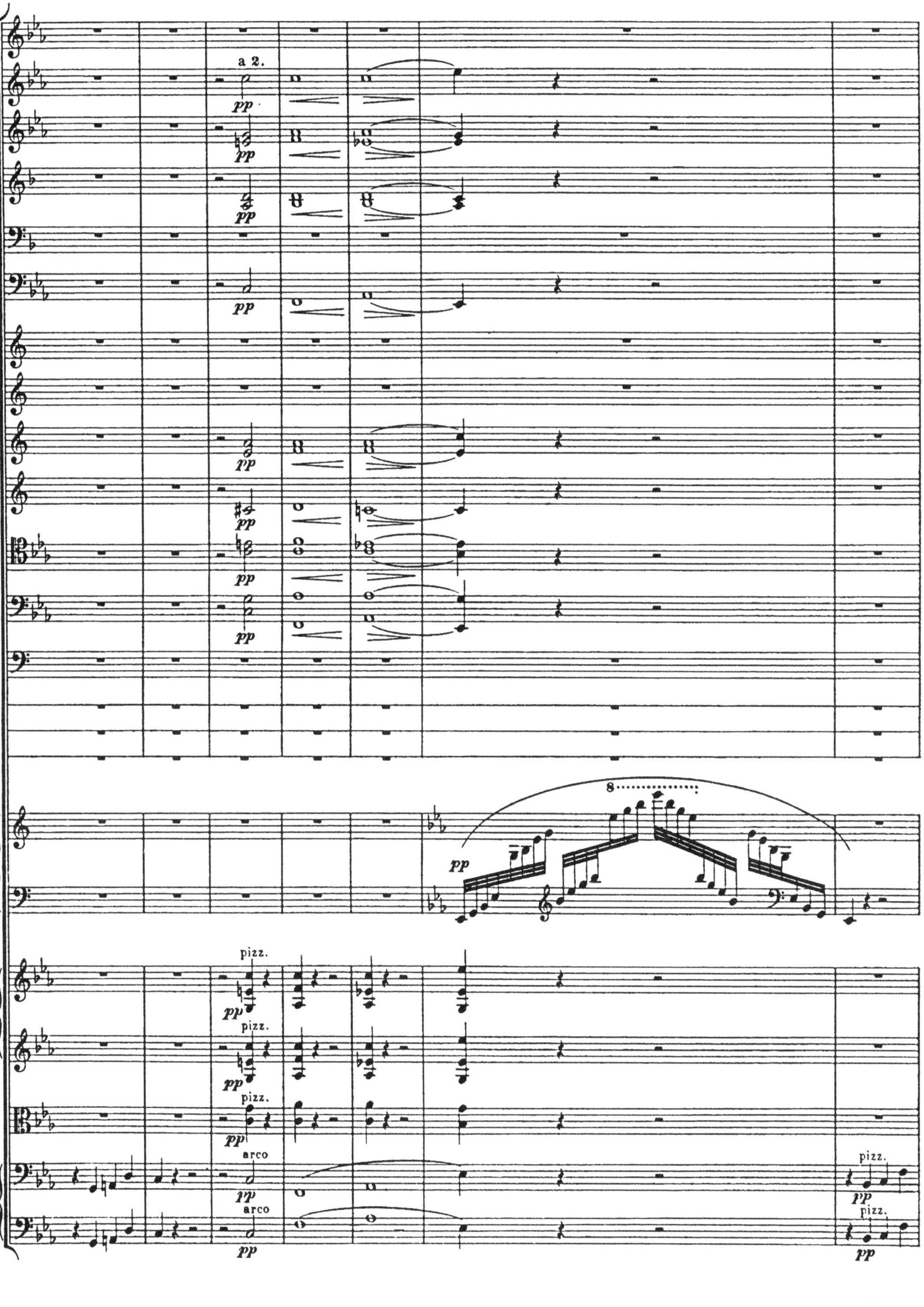
a 2.
pp
pizz.
arco
8

146

ritenuto

ritenuto   pp

F. L. 1.

FRANZ LISZTS
SYMPHONISCHE DICHTUNGEN 1 u. 2

REVISIONSBERICHT

Im Jahre 1908 wurden in einer gemeinschaftlichen Sitzung der Revisoren, der Herausgeber und der Verleger die Leitgedanken und Grundsätze für eine vollständige, einheitliche und korrekte Gesamtausgabe der Werke Franz Liszts beraten und endgültig festgesetzt.

Aus praktischen Gründen der modernen Musikpflege mußten die vielfachen Unterschiede in der Benennung und Anordnung der Instrumente, in den Schlüsseln usw., vor allem aber sehr viele, für heutige Begriffe überflüssige oder selbst störende Versetzungszeichen beseitigt werden. Die auf letztere bezügliche Bestimmung lautet in endgültiger Fassung:

»Die von Liszt sehr reichlich angewendeten zufälligen Versetzungszeichen (namentlich Auflösungszeichen) sind für die heutige Praxis zum Teil entbehrlich geworden. Die nicht unbedingt notwendigen sind nur da beizubehalten, wo sie das Lesen tatsächlich noch erleichtern, Mißverständnisse verhüten oder für das harmonische Bild Lisztscher Schreibweise besonders charakteristisch erscheinen.«

Um jede Willkür auszuschliessen, sind alle irgendwie nennenswerten Änderungen, Weglassungen, Zusätze im Wortlaut der Lisztschen Partitur im Revisionsbericht je bei der betreffenden Komposition besonders aufgeführt und begründet worden, sodaß jeder mit der alten und der neuen Ausgabe in der Hand sich sein Urteil selbst bilden kann. Alle Zutaten, insbesondere Vortragsbezeichnungen, wurden in Klammern ( ) oder [ ] gesetzt; in einzelnen Fällen kann und soll dies nachträglich noch geschehen.

Die Herausgabe der Symphonischen Dichtungen war ursprünglich von Herrn Eugen d'Albert übernommen worden, der jedoch wegen anderweitiger großer Inanspruchnahme zurücktrat, nachdem er den Stich aller 12 Werke nur in erster Lesung hatte beaufsichtigen können. Die genaue Nachprüfung übernahm in dankenswerter Weise Herr Otto Taubmann in Berlin, in stetem Einvernehmen mit dem Kustos des Liszt-Museums, Herrn Hofrat Dr. Obrist, als dem Obmann der Revisionskommission.

BAND 1

CE QU'ON ENTEND SUR LA MONTAGNE.

Symphonische Dichtung Nr. 1*).

Vorlage: 1. Die erste Partiturausgabe, erschienen 1857 bei Breitkopf & Härtel in Leipzig. Verlagsnummer 9382.

2. Die autographe Partitur im Liszt-Museum in Weimar. Diese Originalhandschrift bot jedoch keine Grundlage für die Revision, da sie erheblich von der gestochenen Partitur abweicht. Liszt hat offenbar später vor dem Druck wesentliche Änderungen vorgenommen.

Bemerkungen:

S. 8. In der gedruckten Vorlage fehlen bei den Hörnern vom 4. zum 5. Takt die Bögen, die sich an derselben Stelle bei Hoboen und Fagotten finden. Als vermutlich versehentlich fortgelassen wurden diese Bögen hinzugefügt.

S. 10. Das *Crescendo* der gr. Trommel führt in der gedruckten Vorlage nicht zu einem dynamischen Höhepunkt. Als solcher wurde die ganze Note im 3. Takt angenommen und der erreichte Stärkegrad durch ein hinzugefügtes *mf* näher bezeichnet.

S. 39. Das 3. Horn hat in der gedruckten Vorlage im 2. Takt und im 8. Takt die Vorschrift »gestopft«. Da anzunehmen ist, daß die ganze Stelle gestopft zu blasen ist, wurde die zweite Vorschrift als irreführend gestrichen.

S. 41 Die gedruckte Vorlage hat für die 3. Posaune im 3. bis 6. Takt nach dem Buchstaben I die von allen anderen Instrumenten abweichende Vortragsbezeichnung:

Das wurde in Übereinstimmung mit der sonstigen Bezeichnung dieser Stelle geändert in:

S. 91. In der gedruckten Vorlage findet sich hier die Anmerkung: »Die Hörner-, Trompeten- und Posaunen-Fanfaren mäßig, aber nicht roh.« Da das Wort »mäßig« keinen verständlichen Sinn ergibt, wurde angenommen, daß es »massig« (engl. »prominent«, frz. »très-sonore«) heiße und ein Druckfehler vorliege.

* * *

---

*) Die in diesem Berichte zu den Symphonischen Dichtungen Nr. 1 bis 4 (erster und zweiter Band der Gesamtausgabe der Symphonischen Dichtungen) gemachten Bemerkungen haben auf die vorliegende Gestalt der genannten Werke keinen Bezug, da beide Bände bereits veröffentlicht waren, als eine Nachprüfung ihres Inhalts im Sinne der für die Gesamtausgabe maßgebenden Leitsätze zu jenen Bemerkungen Anlaß gab. Die betreffenden Änderungen können erst bei einem etwaigen Neudruck in die Platten eingetragen werden.
Otto Taubmann.

TASSO, LAMENTO E TRIONFO.

Symphonische Dichtung Nr. 2.

Vorlage: Die erste Partiturausgabe, erschienen 1856 bei Breitkopf & Härtel in Leipzig. Verlagsnummer 9136.

Bemerkungen:

S. 1. Auf Seite 177 der 1885 erschienenen Bandausgabe (Symphonische Dichtungen Nr. 1 bis 4, Volksausgabe Breitkopf & Härtel Nr. 517) findet sich folgende Bemerkung des Komponisten: Der Schluß-Satz kann ohne das Vorhergehende von Seite 223 Buchstabe H *Allegro con molto brio*, separat aufgeführt werden.

S. 1. Es dürfte interessieren, daß Liszt hier ganz ausnahmsweise ausdrücklich 2 Ventiltrompeten vorgeschrieben hat.

S. 4. In der gedruckten Vorlage fehlt für Einsatz der Streicher und der Hoboe im letzten Takt die Angabe des Stärkegrades. Im Hinblick auf die Angabe »*mf*« der Vorlage für Flöte und Klarinette im 4. Takt auf S. 5 erhielten auch die oben genannten Instrumente ein »*mf*«.

S. 6. Der Deutlichkeit wegen erhielten die Rhythmen ♩♪ der Violinen und Bratschen im 1. bis 4. Takt die in der Vorlage nicht enthaltene Form ♩ · ♪.

S. 9. In der gedruckten Vorlage steht bei den Streichern vom 3. Takte an die Vorschrift »*cresc. e sempre più agitato e stringendo*«; bei den Bläsern fehlt diese Vorschrift. Da sie sich auf den Vortrag der ganzen Stelle bezieht, wurde sie über und unter das Gesamtsystem der Partitur gesetzt, bei den Streichern jedoch entfernt. Die Vorschrift »*ed agitato*« bei den Bläsern auf S. 10, 2. Takt wurde dadurch überflüssig gemacht und gleichfalls weggelassen.

S. 12 hat die gedruckte Vorlage im 6. Takt bei der Klarinette ein »*rit.*«, das durch die gleichzeitige Angabe *ritard.* über und unter dem Gesamtsystem der Partitur als überflüssig erschien und deshalb gestrichen wurde.

S. 17. Die gedruckte Vorlage hat im letzten Takt bei Violoncell I die Bezeichnung »Solo«. Da es sich hier augenscheinlich nicht um die Wiedergabe der Stelle durch ein Violoncello, sondern vielmehr um den solistischen Vortrag der Kantilene durch alle ersten Violoncelle handelt, wurde die irreführende Bezeichnung gestrichen.

S. 55, 5. Takt ff. Hier lag der bei S. 9 erwähnte Fall vor, der in gleicher Weise behandelt wurde.

S. 59. In der gedruckten Vorlage ist die Taktart für das *Allegro con molto brio* (Buchstabe H) mit C angegeben. Dagegen hat Liszts erstes Manuskript ₵. Demgemäß ist die Angabe der Vorlage in ₵ geändert worden.

* * *

www.ingramcontent.com/pod-product-compliance
Lightning Source LLC
Chambersburg PA
CBHW080511110426
42742CB00017B/3079